APPLIED PROFESSIONAL ETHICS

A Developmental Approach for Use with Case Studies

Gregory R. Beabout
Saint Louis University

Daryl J. Wennemann
Fontbonne College

UNIVERSITY PRESS OF AMERICA

Lanham • New York • London

University Press of America®, Inc.
4501 Forbes Boulevard, Suite 200
Lanham, Maryland 20706

3 Henrietta Street
London WC2E 8LU England

Printed in the United States of America
British Cataloging in Publication Information Available

Library of Congress Cataloging-in-Publication Data

Beabout, Gregory R.
Applied professional ethics : a developmental approach for use with case studies / Gregory R. Beabout, Daryl J. Wennemann.
p. cm.
Includes bibliographical references.
1. Professional ethics. 2. Moral development.
I. Wennemann, Daryl J. II. Title.
BJ1725.B33 1994 174—dc20 93–39775 CIP

ISBN 0–8191–9373–9 (cloth : alk. paper)
ISBN 0–8191–9374–7 (pbk. : alk. paper)

™ The paper used in this publication meets the minimum requirements of American National Standard for Information Sciences—Permanence of Paper for Printed Library Materials, ANSI Z39.48–1984.

To

Cindy, Cheryl and our families

Contents

List of Diagrams

Preface

This book is written for students. It grew out of our experience teaching applied ethics in pre-professional programs.

The goal of our book is to provide a bare bones, understandable framework for applied professional ethics. It is intended to be used in conjunction with case studies.

Our hope was to make the book readable and accessible to college level students. We do not assume a technical background in philosophy or ethics. Our compact style allows us to set forth and explain a sound framework for professional ethics that students can quickly put into practice in analyzing and writing about cases, leading the student directly and effectively from a theoretical framework to applied ethics and decision-making.

This book is intended to be used in any course that treats the ethical component of professional life through case studies. These include medical ethics, business ethics, engineering ethics, legal ethics, and others. Because of the book's small size, it could be used as a supplemental text in any course that uses the case study approach. Increasingly, professional organizations and accrediting agencies are calling for teaching ethics as an integral component of technical courses, rather than simply as a separate course offered by the philosophy department. For example, the Accreditation Board for Engineering and Technology is interested in having engineering students do more than take a course in ethics. They want them to study the ethical components of their profession in their engineering and design courses. While the book is well suited for philosophy courses in applied ethics, we hope that it will move out of the confines of philosophy departments, and even out of academia, to be used in corporate seminars and presentations as well.

Our book uses Kohlberg's theory to describe the structure of moral development and shows how it applies to professional life. We draw on the insights of Carol Gilligan to show how her ethic of care can yield a fuller understanding of the principle of respect for persons. After setting forth and explaining seven basic moral principles for professional life, we provide a three step system for applying those principles. There is a chapter on the healthy use of conflict and dialogue, and a chapter on context and character. Appendices include Codes of Professional Ethics, How to Write a Case Study Report, Examples of Student Case Study Reports, Works on Moral Theory, and Works that Contain Case Studies.

G.R.B
D.J.W.

St. Louis, Missouri
1993

Acknowledgements

In the spring of 1990, we were discussing our ethics classes with one another, and we found that we shared many of the same frustrations and complaints about the textbooks that we were using. Our primary disappointment was that the textbooks that were available seemed to be written by professional ethicians for professional ethicians, and that many of our students were not reached by the abstract issues of meta-ethics covered in their books. We began discussing ideas for an approach that would touch their lives. This book is the result.

We would like to thank our students at Saint Louis University, Fontbonne College, Parks College, Deaconess College of Nursing, St. Thomas Aquinas College, Milwaukee Area Technical College, Cardinal Stritch College, and Marquette University. Their questions and insights have helped us understand the task of this book and then develop the ideas through various drafts that we have used in our teaching.

In addition to a number of reviewers, we need to thank our friends and colleagues who have read drafts of the text and made helpful suggestions. These include Michael Barry from Albion College, Scott Beallis, D.D.S., Cindy Beabout, Douglas Henson from Mayo Clinic and Thomas Walsh from Saint Louis University. We are grateful for the encouragement we received from the participants in the National Conference on Ethics and the Professions held at the University of Florida in 1992.

We owe a special debt of thanks to John Morris, our graduate assistant, to Edward J. Sabin for his encouragement and support of our project, and to Parks College for providing funding and release time.

Introduction

This book is written for professionals and pre-professionals. It is intended to be used in conjunction with case studies.

Of course, all of us come to the study of applied professional ethics with a degree of ethical experience. In your family, you learned right from wrong. Your teachers have extended your ability to make good judgments. And others in society have provided examples of ethical ideals.

However, you may not have a clear understanding of your moral experiences, especially if you don't often reflect on them. Many people have notions of right and wrong that may be vague, shrouded in ill-defined feelings or emotions. This is often expressed in moral judgments: "I just feel this is wrong. I don't know why, but that's how I feel."

The study of ethics extends our ordinary moral experience, but makes it explicit, clearer, and more consistent. It should help us to give articulate, defensible reasons for why certain actions ought or ought not be done.

Ethics, then, is the study of how to live life well. It includes a reflection on the process of moral development and different kinds of moral reasoning. It studies actions in order to determine what principles should guide them and to evaluate whether specific actions are permissible, impermissible or obligatory. This includes the study of human conduct, social norms, right and wrong.

Ethics also focuses on agents, that is, persons who carry out actions. Here one of the central concerns is on the character traits that shape actions. Is the person acting virtuously, showing care, being responsible? How responsible is the person for the action?

Our goal in this book is to provide an understandable framework for applied professional ethics, one that is simple but not simplistic. The framework should be accessible and relatively easy to apply, because the cases faced by contemporary professionals are often complicated and controversial. It does not help to have complicated philosophical jargon on top of controversial moral issues. One common pitfall is to create special philosophical tools out of the most difficult, complicated cases. These are not the kinds of cases that most professionals will commonly face. That is why we have set forth a straightforward framework for moral reasoning.

In our experience, the most beneficial results of a course in applied professional ethics are to provide an orderly way of thinking about ethics and a common moral vocabulary. The worst thing ethics courses can do is to leave students feeling morally disoriented, with an overly complicated framework only partially understood, and a collection of cases that seem unsolvable.

Many books that address applied ethics lack a coherent structure in their presentation of moral principles.[1] This may result in a certain degree of confusion on the part of the student. One student in an applied ethics course wrote in the course evaluation, "I learned there was no such thing as right and wrong, just good and bad arguments."[2] Without a consistent structure that orders moral principles, moral rules tend to be applied haphazardly. It is not uncommon for a student, for example, to follow John Rawls on affirmative action, John Stuart Mill on allocation of scarce resources and Immanuel Kant on the problem of paternalism in medical decision-making. So one problem with current books on applied ethics is that they lead to an arbitrary application of principles.

Another related problem is that the potpourri of moral principles offered in such texts reinforces an unhelpful sense of moral relativism.[3] For example, Velasquez's book on business ethics,[4] Munson's book on medical ethics,[5] and Martin and Schinzinger's book on engineering ethics all follow the same format.[6] First, a list of competing moral theories and principles is provided. Then, with respect to each moral issue, the authors apply varying moral judgments that may follow from these diverse principles. One is left with the sense that all positions are of equal weight. This approach does not address the problem of applied ethics. The student already knows that there are various views on these issues. In fact, many students will say that "what is right is what you think is right." The potpourri approach merely provides a new, jargon-filled vocabulary to express this attitude. But applied ethics ought to do more. It should contribute to resolving contemporary moral dilemmas by providing a coherent structure of moral principles and a common moral vocabulary. In short, it should make it clear that some ways of thinking and acting are better than others.

The framework and principles that we set forth can be applied in any of the areas of professional ethics. There is a tendency to think that there is a special ethic for each of the various professions, that medical ethics is different than business ethics or engineering ethics. This specialized approach presupposes that the medical community is its own closed society with its own ethical norms, as is every other profession. A fuller understanding of ethics includes all human activities, so that medical ethics is a part of the ethical life, as is business ethics, engineering ethics and so on. The same general moral framework and vocabulary that is used in one profession can be fruitfully applied in another.

Of course, there are problems that are peculiar to each profession, so that when ethics is applied to a particular profession, principles that are specific to that profession come into play. For example, the codes of ethics of the various professions specify ethical norms germane to each. Still, they can be fruitfully understood as flowing from a common source. Both physicians and accountants need a general framework that allows them to make sense of honesty and confidentiality in their professional activity. The same broad moral principles apply, though the particular circumstances of each profession may differ in determining how they apply.

This book is intended to be used along with case studies. The case study method is popular because it provides concrete examples for applying moral principles. It also involves students in the active development of moral prudence as it pertains to their professional expertise.[7] This approach is widely used in medical, engineering, business and legal ethics. Sometimes case studies textbooks (or professors' collections of cases) are presented without first providing a coherent account of moral principles. For example, in Pence's *Classic Cases in Medical Ethics*, though the student is given a good explanation of each case, there is no overarching framework provided to reach solutions.[8]

In our experience, this book works well as a bridge connecting theory and practice. It is usually best for students to get the broad theoretical picture before focusing on application. An ethics course might begin with primary source material such as Plato, Aristotle, Mill, and Kant, and then turn to our book for a synthesis that prepares the student for applied ethics. A medical ethics course might begin with an examination of the social context in which advancing technology shapes medical practice, such as Ivan Illich's *Medical Nemesis*. A business ethics course might open using E.F. Schumacher's *Small is Beautiful: Economics as if People Mattered* which explores ways in which ethical norms are implicit in economic decisions. In an engineering ethics course, students might first read Samuel Florman's *The Civilized Engineer* which addresses broad social questions about the role of engineering in contemporary society. After the student has examined the theoretical setting or the broad social background in which one's future profession is placed, one can then use this book to acquire a framework and vocabulary for working through case studies.

Our claim is that Lawrence Kohlberg's theory of moral development can provide structure to the presentation of moral principles. A number of recent books on applied ethics make use of Kohlberg's theory, but they often use his theory simply to explain the way people think and act. We go farther. We use Kohlberg's theory to show how professionals should make good moral decisions, and why. Kohlberg's model can also contribute to resolving conflicts between interests, roles and principles. Using Kohlberg's theory, we want to recognize a plurality of moral perspectives but show that they can be hierarchically arranged in order to give some concerns priority over others.

One advantage to the organization of moral principles that we set forth is that the main organizing principle, the ideal of respect for each person as an individual, is readily accessible. While the concept of respect for persons is not essentially religious in character, it is one that many students from diverse religious traditions seem to identify with very strongly. In our experience teaching applied ethics, we have encountered students from a number of religious traditions including Christianity, Judaism, Islam, Hinduism and Buddhism, as well as students who do not identify with any particular religious tradition. On a number of occasions, students have said that the fundamental principle that we set forth here, the idea of respect for persons, is consonant with their religious training. However, without a clear understanding of rational moral principles derived from common experience, morality tends to be seen as a matter of private religious belief. The principle of respect for persons will help religious people knit their central moral beliefs into the fabric of a common public morality befitting professionals.[9] The moral life ought to be made of whole cloth. The study of applied professional ethics that focuses on moral principles should not be carried out in a vacuum. The challenge of such a study is to help develop a balance between the diverse personal interests, social roles and moral principles encountered by professionals.

Another advantage to the hierarchy of moral principles suggested by Kohlberg's studies is that it helps to resolve two debates. First, it can resolve the conflicts between various moral perspectives that are generally recognized as significant in moral decision-making. For example, we will claim that the principle of respect for persons has priority over the principle of utility. So, in reasoning about the allocation of scarce medical resources, we should choose a course of action that has the best consequences, but not at the expense of intentionally violating an individual's dignity.

The second debate that needs resolution concerns the conflict between rules and relationships. Carol Gilligan has challenged Kohlberg's model of moral development. Her claim is that Kohlberg's studies favor males since he overemphasizes rules. Her studies of females, published under the title *In Another Voice*, suggest that there is another model of moral development where relationships are more important than rules.[10] At the same time, Alasdair MacIntyre has argued that moral theories that focus on rules, such as those of Kant and Mill, lead to conflicts that are unresolvable without reference to human character and relationships.[11] So both Gilligan and MacIntyre would agree that rules without relationships yield a morality without content.

While we will agree with Gilligan and MacIntyre that matters of human character and relationships are primary in our moral experience, relationships without principles can yield a blind morality.[12] Not all human relationships are healthy.[13] Moral principles can serve to provide a critical test for actions that form our character and relationships. We have constructed this text so that students can read it in one or two sittings. After an initial reading, it can be used for reference in applying principles to cases, both in the classroom and in professional settings.

The aim of the book, then, is to provide professionals a coherent moral framework within which they can develop prudence by gaining practice in applying principles to concrete moral problems that they may face in their professional lives. This activity contributes to the formation of moral character by applying moral principles in light of personal relationships that foster human dignity.

Notes to Introduction

1. For example, see Ronald Munson, *Intervention and Reflection: Basic Issues in Medical Ethics*. Third Edition. (New York: Wadsworth, 1988).

2. Christina Sommers encountered this reaction from one of her students. See her article "Teaching the Virtues," in *The American Philosophical Association's Newsletter on Teaching Philosophy*, Winter 1991, Volume 90:2, p. 42.

3."Our responsibility as teachers goes beyond purveying information about the leading ethical theories and in developing dialectical skill in moral casuistry. I have come to see that dilemma ethics is especially lacking in edificatory force and indeed that it may even be a significant factor in encouraging a superficial moral relativism." *Ibid.*, p. 43.

4. Manuel G. Velasquez, *Business Ethics: Concepts and Cases*. (Englewood Cliffs: Prentice Hall, 1982).

5. *Op. cit.*

6. Mike W. Martin and Roland Schinzinger, *Ethics in Engineering*. (New York: McGraw-Hill, 1983).

7. Prudence is the practical wisdom that allows one to apply moral principles to concrete cases. See Chapter 5.

8. Gregory E. Pence, *Classic Cases in Medical Ethics*. (New York: McGraw-Hill, 1990). Also, see Terrence F. Ackerman and Carson Strong, *A Casebook of Medical Ethics*. (New York: Oxford University Press, 1989).

9. The problem of establishing a common moral discourse is described in Bellah's *Habits of the Heart*, (New York: Perennial Library, 1985), and in *The Good Society*, (New York: Alfred A. Knopf, 1991).

10. Carol Gilligan, *In Another Voice: Psychological Theory and Women's Development*. (Cambridge: Harvard University Press, 1982).

11. Alasdair MacIntyre, *After Virtue: A Study in Moral Theory*. Second Edition. (Notre Dame: University of Notre Dame Press, 1984).

12. Gregory Pence's *Ethical Options in Medicine*. (Oradell, NJ: Medical Economics Co., 1980) is an example of a book that focuses on relationships and character in professional applied ethics rather than providing a strict formulation of rules or principles. The last chapter is titled "Relationships and Virtues."

13. For example, consider the recent work on co-dependency. See Melody Beattie, *CoDependent No More: How to Stop Controlling Others and Start Caring for Yourself*. (New York: HarperCollins, 1987).

Chapter 1

What is Ethics?

Some people use the terms "morality" and "ethics" to mean a system of values. As Alan Donagan writes, "There is a usage, advocated by Nietzsche, and now standard in sociology, according to which any system of mores is a morality."[1] If this were the case, then ethics would simply be the study of systems of values. Ethical theory would describe the mores and values that guide the behavior of individuals or members of a given group. For example, the Amish have a system of values that is drastically different from mainstream American culture. When ethics and morality are understood in this sense, then these two groups have different ethics, two moralities that are incommensurable.

But this is not what we mean by ethics. As we have stated in the Introduction, ethics is the study of how to live life well. It includes both ethical theory and application. While we are primarily concerned with applied ethics, a certain familiarity with ethical theory will be helpful. Ethical theory involves determining the standard by which systems of mores are to be judged.[2] So when ethicists talk about a theory of ethics, they are concerned with determining what standard should be used to evaluate the morality of actions, and determining how to order competing standards. Of course, different ethicians have different theories of what the standard is. Let's look at several of the most prominent standards.

Prominent Theories of Ethics

1. Egoism.

Egoism is the view that the standard that should be used to determine the best course of action is self-interest. Choose the course of action that produces the most individual pleasure and avoids the most pain. While young children seem to almost naturally act according to this principle, it has been espoused by some serious thinkers and philosophers. They hold that it is a fact of human psychology that people always act out of self-interest. This view, called psychological egoism, claims to be an accurate description of how people act. Some people hold that this psychological description of how people act is true, and they use it as a basis for a normative theory called ethical egoism. Ethical egoism states that an action is right if it promotes one's own self-interest. Plato wrote of a character in ancient Greece named Callicles who argued that the good life is found in following your own desires. Ayn Rand wrote of *The Virtue of Selfishness*. In her work, Rand elevates the principle of egoism to the level of a philosophical ethic. The philosophy of egoism is given popular expression by the lead character in the film *Wall Street* when he argues that "greed is good." So egoism places self-interest at the center of the moral life.

2. Conventional Morality.

Conventional morality states that the standard for determining right and wrong is the customary rules or practices of one's society. It has been a widely held view, even since Ancient Greece when the sophist Gorgias held that the key to the moral life is to live up to the expectations of others in society. This view is opposed to egoism, in the sense that it postpones immediate self-interest and urges a concern for the welfare of the group. Conventional morality claims that a person's long term self-interest lies in maintaining conventional or traditional social standards.

3. Utilitarianism

Another prominent ethical theory states that the standard used to determine the morality of an action is the principle of utility. This principle states that one should choose the course of action that produces the greatest benefit for the greatest number of people. In other words, an action is right if it is useful. By focusing on the benefits, utilitarianism is concerned primarily with the consequences of action. Two of the most famous proponents of this theory are Jeremy Bentham (1748-1832) and John Stuart Mill (1806-73). Each argued that the standard for judging actions should be the principle of utility.

Contemporary utilitarians have distinguished two versions of the principle of utility. *Act utilitarianism* states that in each circumstance, one should choose the action that produces the greatest amount of good for the greatest number of people. Because the circumstances of each action are unique, it is necessary to apply the principle to every specific action. In most circumstances, lying or stealing may have bad consequences. But act utilitarianism implies that such acts may be occasionally warranted because of their effects. In fact, any action could be beneficial under the right circumstances.

Rule utilitarianism recognizes that it is virtually impossible to accurately predict the consequences of every single action. In a difficult situation, it may look as if lying will have the best outcome, but then it turns out to be worse than first suspected. You may be caught in a lie, and then you would lose the trust of others. Recognizing these problems, rule utilitarianism states that in each circumstance, one should follow the rule that produces the greatest amount of good for the greatest number of people. In general, stealing produces more harm than good. So the rule is that stealing is wrong. Even if it would happen that a given act of stealing produced good consequences, rule utilitarianism states that one should follow the rule.

4. Duty Ethics.

Some ethicists place duty as the ultimate standard. According to this approach, a morally right action is one that is done solely for the sake of duty. A business person may act in accord with duty, for example, by always being careful not to overcharge customers. However, the motive for such behavior may in fact be expedience, on the grounds that honesty is the best policy. Or the motive may be fear of getting caught with its consequent shame. If duty is the ultimate standard of morality, then a moral action is one motivated by duty. This is what it means to act for the sake of duty. The business person who acts for the sake of duty does so not because of self-interest or because it is socially expected, but because it is one's moral duty. This approach is called a deontological theory. It is identified with the moral theory of Immanuel Kant (1724-1804).

In his *Foundations of the Metaphysics of Morals*, Kant develops the idea of a categorical imperative. A categorical imperative is a command of practical reason that is universal and necessary. In other words, the command is a moral norm that applies to the actions of all rational beings and is morally binding. The categorical imperative is unconditionally necessary; I don't do the right thing to get a raise or to look good in the eyes of others, but because I have committed myself to acting according to the moral law. Although Kant thinks that there is only one such imperative, he presents four versions of it. The first and third are the most famous. Kant's first formulation of the categorical imperative is:

> Act only according to that maxim by which you can at the same time will that it should become a universal law.[3]

The main idea in this formulation is the idea of universalizability. Suppose you are tempted to lie in order to complete a business transaction. To test whether this action is morally permissible, one would attempt to universalize the maxim "one should lie." If it is a moral maxim, it can be applied consistently. If all business people adopted this law, then no business transactions could be completed. Since it cannot be applied consistently, it is not a moral law. Therefore, it is a moral duty to refrain from lying.

Another famous formulation of the categorical imperative states:

> Act so that you treat humanity, whether in your own person or in that of another, always as an end, and never as a means only.[4]

The main idea in this version is the idea of respect for persons. To treat someone as a means only is to treat them as an object, that is, to use them. For example, if you enslave someone to pick your crops, you are treating them as a means only. To treat someone as an end, as a rational being free to make their own choices, is to treat them with the respect befitting a human being. It is possible to treat someone as both a means and an end. For example, if you hire someone to pick your crops, paying them a fair wage and providing decent working conditions, you are treating them as both a means and as an end. This version of the categorical imperative states that it is one's duty to treat all human beings with respect.

5. Virtue Ethics.

Some ethicians claim that virtue is the most important element in the moral life. This approach has its roots in the ethical theories of Plato and Aristotle. It was further developed in the medieval natural law tradition. For such thinkers, ethics means developing virtues such as wisdom, justice, temperance and prudence. The good life consists in forming good habits of character. Aristotle describes virtue as a state of character produced by habit that avoids extremes by aiming at moderation.[5] Such a state of character helps make a human being good and to perform one's function well. Alasdair MacIntyre, in his book *After Virtue*, argues that Aristotle is correct in placing primary emphasis on virtue in the moral life. By emphasizing virtue, the moral life involves more than following abstract norms such as utility or duty. The virtues are habits that bring about self-actualization so that one can flourish as a human being. This self-actualization goes beyond a selfish concern for personal pleasure by including the aspiration for social goods and healthy human relationships. Martin Buber, the Jewish philosopher, expressed this notion of self-actualization when he said that in the afterlife, when he faces his judgment, he won't be asked "Why weren't you more like Moses?" Rather, he will be asked "Why weren't you more like Martin Buber?"

Problems with These Prominent Theories of Ethics

It is commonly recognized that each of these theories have several problems. Examining the problems with each of these theories will be helpful so that we can turn to a more suitable framework for applied professional ethics.

1. Problems with Egoism.

Egoism places self-interest as the fundamental standard of morality. The problem with this approach is not only that its adherents end up being selfish, but that it can not be consistently applied. Anyone who tries to live a life of self-interest finds out that they have incompatible interests. One of the most common practical moral problems that people face is a conflict of interest. This occurs when two or more interests conflict. It often involves a conflict between integrity and financial gain. It is in your own self-interest to maintain integrity, so that people will trust you in the future. But it is also in your self-interest to do whatever is necessary to financially enrich yourself. If the standard used to determine the best course of action is self-interest, then there is no way in principle to make a decision in such cases.

Further, the serious egoist finds that one's self-interest entails having friends and relations that one can rely on in times of need. Therefore, it is in one's self-interest to be concerned with the interest of others. But being concerned with the interest of others sometimes requires subordinating self-interest to their interests. Parents who have helped care for a sick child through sleepless nights know that the self-interest of raising a child turns into a selfless concern for another. In the movie Rain Man, the character played by Tom Cruise is at first motivated simply by self-interest, since it is in his self-interest to take care of an autistic-savant brother. But his self-interest in insuring that he will get his inheritance becomes a selfless concern for the welfare of his brother.

2. Problems with Conventional Morality.

Conventional morality follows the customary rules and practices of one's society in determining right and wrong. The problem with this approach is that you may find yourself living in a morally corrupt society. Would you consider the social standards of Nazi Germany to be morally acceptable? This is an extreme example, but it shows that simple conformity to social standards is inadequate as a standard of ethics. Even the conventional values of middle class American society are not without problems. They may support social inequalities in the form of glass barriers. There are subtle patterns of discrimination that remain invisible to those who unquestioningly accept contemporary conventional standards. Furthermore, it took many years of social criticism directed against the status quo for the mainstream culture to embrace environmental considerations.

3. Problems with Utilitarianism.

Utilitarianism is the theory that an action is right in proportion to its consequences, so that one should produce the greatest good for the greatest number of people. There are two main problems with making utility the ultimate standard of morality.

First, by focusing on the consequences, utilitarianism tends to disregard the intention and motive of actions. Consider this example. Suppose there are two assassins. Independently, each plans to kill the president. (Assume that killing the president would have bad consequences.) Assassin A is a sharp shooter. Assassin B is a lousy shot. Standing on opposite sides of the president, both raise their guns and take aim. Assassin B shoots first. The bullet flies past the president and hits Assassin A in the shoulder, knocking the rifle from Assassin A's arms. From the perspective of utility, Assassin B's action had a good consequence, so it was a good action. But it is obvious that Assassin B's action is in fact bad. However, to determine the morality of the action, a different standard must be used, a standard that considers the intention and motive of the action, not just the consequence.

Second, as contemporary utilitarians have explained, all utilitarians are either act utilitarians or rule utilitarians. Act utilitarians hold that in each circumstance, one should choose the action that produces the greatest amount of good for the greatest number of people. However, that assumes that it is possible to accurately predict the consequences of an action in each case. Instead of providing an accurate standard for determining the morality of actions, act utilitarianism is guesswork. Rule utilitarians hold that it is virtually impossible to accurately predict the consequences of every single action, so that in each circumstance, one should follow the rule that produces the greatest amount of good for the greatest number of people. In general, following the rule will produce the greatest good for the greatest number. But in any specific case, following the rule may not produce the best consequences. Therefore, rule utilitarianism is not really utilitarianism, since it makes a rule the standard of actions, and not the consequences. In short, all utilitarians are either act or rule utilitarians. But act utilitarianism is flawed in that it wrongly assumes that the consequences of each act can be accurately predicted. And rule utilitarianism is self-contradictory, since it is not really utilitarianism, but is instead rule worshipping. Therefore, utilitarianism is flawed as the ultimate standard of morality.[6]

4. Problems with Duty Ethics.

Duty ethics is the theory that states that a morally good action is one that is done solely for the sake of duty. There are two main problems with duty ethics. First, the principle of universalizability may be inadequate as the sole standard to determine one's duty. It would seem to be possible to universalize a rule or maxim such as "lie when you can get away with it." So whether a rule can be universalized depends on how the action is described and how detailed the conditions of the action are. If the maxim is formulated with very specific qualifications, then almost any action could be universalized: lie when it helps your company and you are certain you won't get caught. Since almost any action could be described with such detailed qualifications that it could be universalized, the principle of universalizability ends up not being helpful as a standard of duty.

Second, it is possible for two duties to conflict. For example, Jean Paul Sartre relates this dilemma faced by a student of his. In World War II, he had to choose between the duty to defend his country and the duty to care for his ailing mother.[7] Both duties seem to entail an obligation. Similarly, business people may face a conflict between duty to one's company and duty to one's society. But how do we fulfill both duties when they conflict?

5. Problems with Virtue Ethics.

Virtue ethics places primary emphasis on forming good habits of character. This approach also has problems. First, the qualities of character that are considered virtuous seem to vary from culture to culture. In Homeric Greece, courage and strength were considered virtues, but not humility. Aristotle emphasized the classical Greek virtues of justice, temperance, prudence and wisdom, while Thomas Aquinas added faith, hope and love to that list. So what is recognized as a virtue seems to vary from time to time, from culture to culture.

It is also unclear whether the same virtues apply to all people universally. Are the qualities of virtuous men the same as those of virtuous women? Are the virtues befitting a mature, middle aged man identical with those of a young man, or an elderly man? So virtue ethics lacks universality in its application.

Finally, virtue ethics suffers from a lack of clarity when applied to specific issues. In a concrete case, it is often unclear what it means to be virtuous. Suppose a woman enters a hospital with a heart condition. She specifies on an admittance form that she does not want any extraordinary treatment. This means that she is not to be revived. Later, she feels distress, and tells her nurse in private that she wants everything possible done to keep her alive. What is the virtuous thing to do? First, it is unclear which virtue is relevant to the decision. Should the nurse act with courage, benevolence, love? Second, what would the courageous act be? Or the benevolent or loving act? Since it is often unclear how to answer these questions, virtue ethics does not always provide clear guidance.

Conclusion

We have explained five prominent theories of ethics and shown that each one has problems. This is widely recognized among scholars who study ethical theory. In fact, there are whole courses and many books devoted to explaining and criticizing these theories in detail at an abstract, theoretical level. We do not intend to pursue a study of meta-ethics for its own sake, what Kant called "the foundation of the metaphysics of morals." Our focus is on applied ethics. Most professionals are not concerned with understanding all of the subtleties of meta-ethics, nor need they be in order to develop practical decision-making skills.

Most books in applied ethics recognize that there is a plurality of ethical theories, and that each one has shortcomings. After explaining these theories and the problems with each, most texts in applied ethics leave it to the student to forge a coherent framework, combining elements from each theory. For example, in Velasquez's book on business ethics, three prominent moral theories are explained and criticized: utility, rights and justice. Velasquez states that there is "no comprehensive moral theory" that successfully orders the claims of utility, rights and justice.[8] Readers are then invited to forge their own synthesis, combining the strengths of each theory while avoiding their weaknesses. He writes "I hope that I have provided sufficient materials to allow the reader to develop a set of ethical norms that he or she can finally accept as adequate."[9] But with little guidance on how to order the apparently conflicting claims of diverse standards, too great a burden is placed on the shoulders of the students.

Hoffman and Moore's book on business ethics uses the same strategy. They begin by introducing four prominent ethical theories. They conclude that "there may be ways of drawing fruitfully on each theory in constructing a moral framework from which to make judgments."[10] For them, the case study method is used to construct a moral framework. But this seems backwards. Their method calls on students to pull themselves up by their own moral bootstraps. The student must construct a theory in the process of learning how to apply a theory to cases. Our book does what these others say can be done. It offers a moral framework, giving order to the various standards commonly used in applied ethics. This prepares the student to use the case method approach to get practice in applied professional ethics. Without such a framework, the tendency is to come away from the study of applied ethics with new jargon and a familiarity with issues, but lacking a way of ordering standards, a helpful vocabulary or a systematic approach to making moral decisions. So, the case method approach is misapplied in applied professional ethics if its purpose is to construct theories. Rather, the case method approach should help professionals and pre-professionals develop a facility in applying ethical theory to cases.

In order to provide a framework and a vocabulary for applied professional ethics, we will turn to developmental psychology. This will supply data on how to organize elements from various ethical theories in light of the psychology of human moral development.

Questions for Review and Discussion

1. What is the difference between a system of values and an ethical theory?

2. What is ethics?

3. What are examples of various standards used in ethical systems?

4. What is egoism? What problems arise with egoism?

5. What is conventional morality? What problems arise with conventional morality?

6. What is utilitarianism? What is the difference between act and rule utilitarianism? What problems arise with utilitarianism?

7. What is duty ethics? What is the categorical imperative? What problems arise with duty ethics?

8. What is virtue ethics? How does it relate to self-actualization? What problems arise with virtue ethics?

9. Are the various standards of morality incompatible?

Notes to Chapter One

1. Alan Donagan, *The Theory of Morality*. (Chicago: University of Chicago Press, 1977), p. 1.

2. *Ibid*. For our definition of ethics, see p. 1.

3. Immanuel Kant, *Foundations of the Metaphysics of Morals*. Translated by Lewis White Beck. (New York: Library of Liberal Arts, 1959), p. 39.

4. *Ibid*., p. 47.

5. Aristotle, *Nicomachean Ethics*, Book II, Chapter 6.

6. This argument is presented in Donagan's *The Theory of Morality*, pp. 192-99.

7. Jean Paul Sartre, "Existentialism is a Humanism," in *Existentialism from Dostoevsky to Sartre*. Ed. Walter Kaufmann. (Cleveland: Meridian Books, 1956), pp. 295-6.

8. Miguel Velasquez, *Business Ethics Concepts and Cases*. (Englewood Cliffs: Prentice Hall, 1992), p. 105. Velasquez includes an explanation of Kohlberg's theory of moral development in his text. However, he does not show how Kohlberg's theory can be used to help forge a comprehensive ethical framework that orders the competing claims of various standards. Instead, he uses Kohlberg to show how we come to accept moral standards.

9. *Ibid*., pp. viii-ix.

10. W. Michael Hoffman and Jennifer Mills Moore, *Business Ethics: Readings and Cases in Corporate Morality*. Second Edition. (New York: McGraw-Hill, 1990), p. 18.

Chapter 2

The Structure of Moral Development: Interest, Roles, and Principles

As a professional, you will face many difficult moral decisions.

You may encounter a situation like the one that some of the medical doctors in San Jose, California faced. They received a prospectus for a limited partnership in a clinical lab with a projected annual return of 70%. The difficulty in the decision seemed to be a conflict of interest. Meris Laboratories Ltd. based the high projected return "on the assumption that each doctor-investor would become a customer, too - sending to the lab for analysis an average of 31.5 specimens a week."[1]

Another kind of decision you may face might involve what seems to be a conflict between your role as an employee and your role as a professional. Consider the conflict Searle Lawson faced. One year after he graduated with his engineering degree, he found himself in a situation in which he had to decide whether he should meet exact mechanical specifications on a proto-type of a four-rotor brake for an A7D aircraft that his company was building for the Air Force or conform to his employer's pressure to "fudge the data" to avoid cost overruns.[2]

You may be faced with what appears to be a conflict between the standards of your society and those of another. Robert Grohman was president of Levi Strauss International, the company that makes Levi's blue jeans. His company was making "payments" to a foreign official in the hopes that it would speed the delivery of his product. Grohman points out that, "Fashion clothing may lose its value if it is late. Delays can cost you 80 percent. In the Far East, trucks may not run right. Goods just don't seem to make it on to ships. Shipments can fall off cranes."[3] In the United States, such payments are illegal. The company's counsel believed that "the payments were legal in the country where they were made."[4] Grohman had to decide whether his company should continue to make the "payments."[5]

The task they all faced, and the one you will face, is to give order to the *interests*, *roles*, and *moral principles* that govern our lives. Today, all professionals, including health care providers, engineers, lawyers, and business people, need a clear understanding of moral principles that can be applied to their professional situations. Such an understanding can help give order to conflicts that professionals face.

The moral challenges that professionals encounter are diverse. It is not enough to simply focus on self-*interest* alone, or *roles*, or moral *principles*. For this reason, we have drawn upon Kohlberg's model of moral development. It provides a structure that is inclusive of all these dimensions, ordering them according to a hierarchy of moral stages.

Kohlberg's Theory of Moral Development

Lawrence Kohlberg (1927-87) was a developmental psychologist who studied moral development. He was interested in how people make moral decisions. As a research psychologist, he carried out interviews, posing moral dilemmas to a range of people. The most famous dilemma he posed was the "Heinz dilemma":

> In Europe, a woman was near death from a special kind of cancer. There was one drug that the doctors thought might save her. It was a form of radium that a druggist in the same town had recently discovered. The drug was expensive to make, but the druggist was charging ten times what the drug cost him to make. He paid $400 for the radium and charged $4,000 for a small dose of the drug. The sick woman's husband, Heinz, went to everyone he knew to borrow the money and tried every legal means, but he could only get together about $2,000, which is half of what it cost. He told the druggist that his wife was dying, and asked him to sell it cheaper or let him pay later. But the druggist said, "No, I discovered the drug and I'm going to make money from it." So, having tried every legal means, Heinz gets desperate and considers breaking into the man's store to steal the drug for his wife. Should Heinz steal the drug?[6]

Kohlberg recorded not only the answers that those interviewed gave to such dilemmas, but also the reasoning that they used to explain their decisions. He found that there is a recognizable pattern of development. Five year olds answer differently than ten year olds. Adolescents often answer differently than adults. The pattern of development Kohlberg identified is a movement from 1) a concern for self-interest, to 2) conformity to social roles, and finally toward 3) a commitment to moral principles.

Kohlberg identified three broad levels of moral development. Within each level, there are two stages. (For our purposes, we will be focusing on the three levels, and not on the more detailed stages. See Diagram 1 on p. 24 for details of the relation between the stages and the levels.)

Level One

At Level One, the child is primarily interested in himself or herself. Rules are obeyed out of fear of punishment, or because a reward is expected. Doing good means getting a benefit or avoiding pain for oneself. The criterion used for moral decision-making at this level is interest, namely self-interest. Level one is called the "pre-conventional" level of moral judgment because it does not take into account the conventions of society. In response to the Heinz dilemma, the child at this level could decide either to steal or not to steal the drug, but either way the rationale used would be that of self-interest:

> Pro: If you let your wife die, you will get in trouble. You'll be blamed for not spending the money to save her, and there'll be an investigation of you and the druggist for your wife's death.
>
> Con: You shouldn't steal the drug because you'll be caught and sent to jail if you do. If you do get away, your conscience would bother you thinking how the police would catch up with you at any minute.[7]

The Level One response based on self-interest is ambiguous, since the individual has conflicting interests.

Level Two

At Level Two, emphasis shifts away from oneself to concern for one's society. This is therefore called the "conventional" level of

Diagram 1

Kohlberg's Model of

Levels and Stages in Moral Development

LEVELS	STAGES	
Level One Pre-Conventional (Self-Interest)	*Stage 1*:	Obedience and punishment orientation. Obey commands in order to avoid punishment.
	Stage 2:	Naive instrumental hedonism. Obey to obtain rewards, have favors returned.
Level Two Conventional (Social Conformity, Roles)	*Stage 3*:	"Good-boy" morality of maintaining good relations. Orientation to approval and helping others.
	Stage 4:	Authority maintaining morality. Conform to avoid censure by legitimate authorities, with resulting guilt. Regard for earned expectations of others.
Transitional Level	*Stage 4 1/2*:	Recognizes that social standards are relative and arbitrary. Moral decisions are thought to be subjective and personal. Conscience is thought to derive from one's emotional responses.
Level Three Post-Conventional (Moral Principles)	*Stage 5*:	Contractual legalistic orientation. Morality of contract, of individual rights, and of democratically accepted law.
	Stage 6:	Morality of universal principles. Orientation to conscience as a directing agent and to mutual respect and trust.

moral judgment, since decisions are based on conformity to the conventions of one's society. Not everyone moves into this level. But those who do move into Level Two obey rules because they are part of the society. The Level Two person tries to do what is expected by others. Conformity is seen as important, as is concern for fulfilling one's role in society. Good is done to maintain the approval of others, and to show respect for the legitimate authorities. The Level Two person is concerned with living up to the expectations of family, peers, or society. The consequences of action are not as important as fulfilling one's role and maintaining the approval of one's own group. At this level, guilt rather than fear of physical punishment is a motivation. In response to the Heinz dilemma, respondents might say:

> Pro: No one will think you're bad if you steal the drug, but your family will think you're an inhuman husband if you don't. If you let your wife die, you'll never be able to look anybody in the face again.
>
> Con: It isn't just the druggist who will think you're a criminal, everyone else will too. After you steal it, you'll feel bad thinking how you've brought dishonor on your family and yourself; you won't be able to face anyone again.[8]

Because we all have many different social roles that often conflict with each other (employee, parent, professional, citizen) the conventional level of moral judgment is unable to resolve the Heinz dilemma.

Level Three

At Level Three, emphasis shifts away from the norms of one's society to a more universal perspective that recognizes impartial moral principles. This highest level is called the "post-conventional" level, since moral judgments are made based on universal moral principles that transcend any particular social conventions. Kohlberg claims that not everyone moves into this level. Few people attain it before the age of eighteen. And furthermore, this highest level is rarely maintained consistently throughout life. At this level, there is concern for some universally applicable moral standard: for example, the principle of respect for all human beings as individuals. Good is done because it is a matter of conscience to apply a logical, universal standard such as the principle of respect. The principle of respect for persons is a self-chosen criterion of moral decision-making. Further, it can function as a criterion for evaluating the conventions of societies, including one's own.[9]

The principle of respect for persons is reversible. When applied properly, the principle of respect takes into account all people, so that a decision would be morally acceptable even if the roles were reversed.

The post-conventional level contributes to a resolution of the Heinz dilemma. Though it may be illegal for the husband to steal the drug, this law is subordinate to the principle of respect for persons. The druggist should be able to hypothetically reverse roles and see that, based on the principle of respect for persons, life is more important than property. At the same time, this does not eliminate the validity of the law against stealing. It merely subordinates it to a higher standard. Of course, Heinz should first exhaust all legal means of acquiring the drug. But if he is unable to acquire the drug, it may be permissible for him to take it, though he should be prepared to face social sanctions for stealing.[10]

Kohlberg's studies show that moral development proceeds from Level One, which is characterized by egoistic self-interest regardless of other concerns, to Level Two, which is characterized by conformity to social norms. At Level Two, the individual has moved beyond himself or herself to be concerned for others, but the concern for others extends only to one's own group or society. Finally, at the highest level, Level Three, the individual makes moral decisions based on a universal moral principle, like the principle of respect for all persons as individuals having inherent dignity. Since these levels are developmental, the individual at the highest level has experienced the significance and the limitations of moral decision-making at the lower levels. Level Three does not eliminate the significance of self-interest or social norms. Rather, it places them in their proper perspective by subordinating them to the principle of respect.

Moral Development and Professional Life

It is most befitting for professionals to make moral decisions at Level Three. To be a professional includes three ideas:

1) that one has a skill acquired through specialized training,
2) that one can give a rational account of one's own activities, explaining the "whys" and "hows" of one's area of expertise,
3) that one is dedicated to using one's skills for the well-being of others.[11]

All three of these components are necessary ingredients for being a professional. If any of these are missing, then you cannot lay claim to the status of being a professional. Many students who pursue professional training realize that they need to acquire specialized skills. They are sometimes more reluctant to acquire the theoretical background of their area. The one thing many fail to see as a component of being a professional is an understanding of the ethical dimension of professional life.

A professional is more than a person having skills and knowledge. To become a professional, you must dedicate the use of your skills and knowledge to further human dignity. Having acquired specialized skills and knowledge, you are in an advantaged position. Therefore, a professional can not make moral decisions (as a professional) solely from the Level One perspective of self-interest.

Further, the Level Two perspective of conformity to social norms as an ultimate standard is inadequate because some social roles are unjust. The Nazi physician who applies his skills to experiment on live prisoners is acting contrary to his professional obligations (expressed in the Hippocratic Oath), though he may be doing what is socially expected.

Another example of Level Two thinking occurs when a particular profession closes in on itself, becoming a closed society with its own social standards which are taken to be moral norms. For example, when "business ethics" is understood to mean that there is a special ethic for business people, one that is different from the moral norms of other professionals or of the society in general, then the possibility of abuse increases because the norms tend to become self-serving. Professional societies ought not to exist solely for the purpose of protecting their members from the ethical standards that apply to everyone else. Rather than being a haven of privilege, professional societies should work to enhance the moral life of their members. Each profession does not have its own unique ethic. That would mean that the moral norms of medicine would be as different from those of accounting as the mores of the Amish are different from the mores of mainstream Americans. Instead, there is ultimately a single ethic that transcends any of the particular professions. This ethic is applied to varying circumstances and particular problems producing different conclusions within different professional contexts.

To be a professional, then, means to adopt the Level Three perspective of respect for persons. Otherwise, the power of one's specialized skills may be abused, either to one's own advantage, or to the advantage of one's social group. This is the rationale for codes of professional behavior that require high ethical standards.[12]

Kohlberg's theory of moral development allows professionals to take into account their own self-interest and the social significance of their professional activities because it subordinates these considerations to the human significance of professional life. The moral task of professionals, therefore, is not to eliminate or ignore self-interest or social expectations. Rather, their moral task is to seek out an effective balance between these claims in light of a higher claim, that of human dignity.

A Transition Through Relativism

So, Kohlberg's theory suggests that moral development moves through these levels:

> Level One: Self-interest,
> Level Two: Social conformity, roles,
> Level Three: Universal moral principles.

Still, not all people fit neatly into one of these three levels. Some people may make moral decisions primarily from one level, though occasionally adopting the perspective of another level. Kohlberg claims that most adult Americans make moral decisions from Level Two, that is, they usually reason that they should do what is expected of them.

To make the transition from Level Two to Level Three, one must have the insight that social norms differ from one society to another, and even between subcultures within a society. Further, one must see that the norms of one's own society are not necessarily always better than the norms of another society. The full development into Level Three does not occur until one also sees that there must be some universal principle for moral decision-making, a standard that applies to all persons, regardless of their social origin.

Kohlberg also identifies a post-conventional but not yet principled level that he calls Stage 4 1/2. Persons at this level recognize that the standards of their own society are not the ultimate standard. Social standards are seen as relative and arbitrary. The criterion for making moral decisions is thought to be highly subjective and personal. In lieu of a rational principle, conscience is seen as deriving from emotional responses.

This is a particularly important point to remember with regard to college age pre-professionals. As high school students, social conformity is a common concern. There is often a tension between family expectations and peer pressure. When students move from home and enter college, this usually entails questioning the social norms of their adolescence. Out of this questioning comes the insight that social norms are relative and seemingly arbitrary. The attitude of moral relativism adopted at this time represents a transition in moral reasoning.

Professors may see this relativism as an obstacle to teaching professional ethics to pre-professionals. Alan Bloom sees this pervasive relativism as a danger to American society.[13] If this emotive relativism is maintained as a permanent attitude, it may be unhealthy, both individually and to the society at large. It can easily lead to the abuse of professional knowledge and skills at the expense of the well-being of others. But if this attitude of relativism is taken to be a transitional stage in the development of moral reasoning, it may be seen as a necessary step to a more comprehensive moral perspective, one of principled conscience.

The "Fact/Value" Problem

It may seem obvious that Level Three is best. Since the principle of respect for persons is the highest principle in psychological moral development, it seems to follow that it is normative. Because Level Three is highest, isn't it the level that ought to be followed and should be prescribed? This is a common level two inference.

However, some philosophers have recognized a fallacy in this kind of reasoning. David Hume (1711-76) argued that it is not valid to begin a line of reasoning using descriptive terms and then conclude with prescriptive terms. For example, just because Americans eat holding the fork in the right hand does not mean that this is the only way one ought to eat. Just because your house is painted white doesn't mean that it is the color it ought to be painted. There is a tendency to reason that "This is the way it is, so that's how it ought to be." Such an argument moves from a description of "what is" to a normative claim about "what ought to be," from a fact to a value. For example, historical facts about the social roles of women in society are not by themselves sufficient evidence for determining the role that women ought to have.

This same "fact/value" distinction can be used to better understand developmental psychology and its place in applied professional ethics. The fact/value distinction illustrates that we cannot simply state "This is how moral development occurs, so you should operate at Level Three." To immediately jump from a fact of psychology to an ethical prescription is to commit the fallacy of arguing from "is" to "ought."

By itself, psychology is inadequate for determining the standard of morality. Still, it has a positive contribution to make to ethics. Developmental psychology helps us to understand that there are different modes of moral reasoning that correspond to stages and levels of human development. In this way, psychology is a step towards a different line of reasoning, to moral arguments for the normative character of Level Three. Even though it is not valid to argue from fact to value, from is to ought, moral reflection should not occur without any knowledge of the facts of human psychology. Such an approach would detract from the concrete character of applied ethics. Besides, it may turn out that what is, ought to be. Accordingly, we will argue that Level Three is not only the highest level developmentally, but also that the Level Three principle of respect for persons is the ultimate norm in moral decision-making.

Why Level Three is Best

Kohlberg's empirical studies of moral development indicate that moral reasoning does in fact develop through the stages and levels that we have outlined. As we have seen, this does not automatically imply that the higher levels are to be preferred. Just because Level Three comes after Level Two developmentally does not necessarily mean that it is better. After all, senility often follows intellectual maturity, but that does not mean that it is better.

Still, the following four reasons, which are independent of developmental psychology, show that Level Three provides a better standard of morality than either Level One or Level Two.

First, Level Three, the perspective of universal respect for persons, resolves more conflicts in moral reasoning than the lower levels. We will demonstrate how this occurs in the examples in the next section.

Second, Level Three is more inclusive than the lower levels. At Level One, moral decisions are based on one's own interests. At Level Two, moral decisions include the consideration of others in one's group. But only Level Three includes all human beings as being worthy of respect. Therefore, Level Three is more altruistic than the lower levels since it promotes the greatest concern for the well-being of others. Because professionalism implies universal concern, the lower levels are inadequate to meet the requirements of a professional's moral decision-making.

Third, as Kohlberg has noted, it is not possible to understand a higher level of moral reasoning from a lower level, though it is possible to understand the moral reasoning of the lower levels, including their limitations and deficiencies, from Level Three.

Finally, the lower levels lend themselves to abuses of power. This is particularly true for professionals, since they have acquired special skills and knowledge that place them in a position of advantage. The person who makes moral decisions from the Level Three perspective, who acts according to moral principle, will avoid the abuses of power that follow from an unprincipled pursuit of self-interest or an unquestioning conformity to social expectations.

Applications to Conflicts

The developmental model that we have described can contribute to the resolution of moral conflicts like the ones we discussed at the beginning of the chapter.

1. Meris Laboratories: A Conflict of Interest?

In the Meris Laboratories case, in which medical doctors were solicited to become partners in a clinical lab where they would send test samples, there seems to be a conflict of two distinct interests. This is especially true if the case is considered from the Level One perspective of self-interest. Typical Level One responses might be:

> Pro: You should invest in the lab, because it will yield a high return on a minimal investment, and you can guarantee that the lab will have business. "I spent a lot of money getting my medical degree, so why shouldn't I make the most profit that I can?"
>
> Con: You shouldn't invest, because your patients may find out that you have a financial interest in the lab and it could ruin your reputation as a physician. Your whole practice might fold and you would be without a career.

Therefore, viewed from the perspective of Level One, there is no genuine resolution to the conflict. There is no principled way to determine if one interest is more important than another. Just as the Heinz dilemma remained ambiguous for the Level One person, so too does the Meris Laboratories case remain ambiguous if it is construed as a conflict of interest. It would be just as reasonable to decide to invest in the laboratory (being motivated by financial self-interest) as it would be not to invest (being motivated by a desire to have a good reputation, construed as a personal interest).

However, from the conventional level of moral judgment, Level Two, the conflict is not between one interest and another, but between one's self-interest and one's role as a physician. From this perspective, roles carry more moral weight than self-interest. Therefore, a clear judgment can be made that one's financial self-interest should be subordinated to one's role as a physician.

This is precisely the kind of decision that Dr. James Schwade made. He said that he "left private practice when he heard that promoters were signing up doctors as partners in a radiation center near the Miami hospital where he practiced."[14] He saw this practice as a form of "medical racketeering." Some physician-investors threatened to cut off referrals to doctors who did not join the venture.[15] He chose not to buy into a physician-owned laboratory, but instead took a position at a university hospital. In doing so, he did not compromise his professional role for the sake of his own financial interest.

2. Searle Lawson and "Fudging the Data": A Conflict of Roles?

In the Air Force brake case, Searle Lawson found himself in a situation in which he had to decide whether he should meet exact mechanical specifications on a proto-type of a four-rotor brake for an A7D aircraft that his company was building for the Air Force or conform to his employer's pressure to "fudge the data" to avoid cost overruns. There seems to be a conflict between his role as an employee and his role as a professional engineer. This is especially true if the case is considered simply from the Level Two perspective of roles and social conformity. Typical Level Two responses might be:

> Pro: Your role as an employee of the company means that you are expected to do what your superiors ask of you. You should be concerned with the good of the company over and above other considerations. Don't rock the boat. Do what your employer expects of you. Otherwise, you'll come to be known as someone who is not a team player.
>
> Con: Your role as an engineer demands that you meet exact mechanical specifications. According to your specialized training, you are qualified to make judgments about safety according to accepted engineering standards. Other engineers would expect that you would honestly report the data. If you "fudge the data," not only would other engineers look down on you, but you might be barred from membership in the National Society of Professional Engineers.

Therefore, viewed from the perspective of Level Two, there is no genuine resolution to this conflict. There is no principled way to determine if one's role as an employee is more important than one's role as an engineer.

However, a resolution is possible if we remember that to be a professional engineer entails acting according to the post-conventional level of moral judgment, Level Three. At this level, social roles and expectations are subordinated to the universal moral principle of respect for persons. So the conflict is not between one role and another. Rather, the choice is between conforming to the expectations of others and acting with honesty according to the moral principle of respect.

Since being a professional engineer entails the moral demand to dedicate one's skills to the well-being of others, it is clear that Searle Lawson should not "fudge the data."

3. Blue Jeans Abroad: A Conflict of Social Norms?

In the Levi Strauss International case, Robert Grohman had to decide whether to make "payments" to assure delivery of fashion clothing on time. In the U.S., this kind of bribery is illegal, but in some other countries, including those where Grohman was operating, it was not. This case seems to be a conflict between the standards of one society and those of another. This is especially true if the case is considered from the intermediate transitional level of moral relativism, Stage 4 1/2. A typical Stage 4 1/2 response would be:

> When in Rome, do as the Romans. Moral standards are arbitrary and without rational basis. Foreigners shouldn't pay bribes here, because that's not the way we do business. But we shouldn't impose our moral standards on them.

The conflict here is that the bribe giver has no principled way to decide what social standards to follow. It may soothe your conscience to say "When in Rome, do as the Romans," but how does this apply if you are an American in Tokyo on the phone completing a business deal with someone in Saudi Arabia? In a sense, such a person is "in" several societies at the same time. He or she is confronted with incompatible social demands and is left without any consistent basis for decision-making.

Insofar as business people are professionals, they should act according to the post-conventional level of moral reasoning, Level Three. (Hopefully, the conflict between social standards encountered at Stage 4 1/2 will help prompt a development into Level Three that subordinates social standards to the principle of respect.) At Level Three, decisions are made according to the universal principle of respect for persons. Since bribe payments demean human dignity and undermine the relationship of trust required for fair exchange, such "payments" are morally impermissible, even if they are socially accepted.

Viewed from this perspective, the conflict is not between one social standard and another, but between a social standard and a moral principle. So by viewing the case from Level Three, the moral conflict is resolved.

John Noonan, a legal scholar and philosopher who has written a book on this topic titled *Bribes*, claims that hard-core bribery will go the way of slavery. "Bribery today is universally condemned. The Western ideal has been accepted everywhere, though in many places adherence may be more rhetorical than real."[16] So Noonan challenges the popular idea that bribery is now socially acceptable in some countries. Where it is practiced, it is nonetheless recognized as being contrary to moral principles because it undermines the human relationship of trust that is the basis of fair exchange.

The 1977 Foreign Corrupt Practices Act is based on the idea that bribery is morally wrong, even if it is practiced in countries where it is legal. This law is "unique in the history of the world because it makes bribing someone else's government a crime."[17] It applies to the bribe giver rather than the recipient. Just as slavery is wrong, not simply because it is illegal, but because it fails to treat human beings with respect, bribery is morally wrong for similar reasons.

Conclusion

In this chapter, we have shown that Kohlberg's theory of moral development can be applied to professional ethics. Doing so provides a hierarchical structure to give order to the various elements of the moral life. Self-interest is subordinated to social roles and standards, which are in turn subordinated to the principle of respect for persons. There is a place for self-interest and social roles and standards. But this developmental hierarchy allows us to make sense of their significance in light of human dignity.

Questions for Review and Discussion

1. Describe a situation in which someone (real or fictional) made a moral decision from Level One, Level Two, Level Three.

2. At what level of moral decision-making do you most often act?

3. Describe the various self-interests that you have. How might they conflict with each other? Do the same for the various social roles that you have.

4. Analyze the concept of professionalism. Why does professionalism entail acting from Level Three? Which is more important: to maintain professional standards or to give the appearance of maintaining professional standards?

5. If a businessperson made a sale based on deceit, would he or she be acting as a professional?

6. Explain the advantages and disadvantages of moral relativism, stage 4 1/2?

7. Explain how Kohlberg's hierarchy of moral development applies to the Meris Laboratory case, the Air Force Brake case, and the blue jeans case.

Notes to Chapter Two

1. "Congress Puts Doctor-Owned Labs on the Examining Table," *Business Week*. August 29, 1988, p. 36.

2. Velasquez, p. 34. This case has been widely discussed in the literature. For a more detailed description of the case, see *Harpers Magazine*, 244 (April 1972), pp. 45-52. The congressional hearings are published as *Air Force Brake Problem: Hearing Before the Subcommittee on Economy in Government of the Joint Economic Committee, Congress of the United States, Ninety First Congress, First Session*, August 13, 1969. Robert Baum discusses the case in his *Ethics and Engineering Curricula*, (Hastings-on-Hudson, NY: The Hastings Center, 1980), p. 58, as well as by John H. Fielder, "Give Goodrich a Break," *Business & Professional Ethics Journal*, vol. 7, No. 1, pp. 3-25.

3. "An Unscandalized View of Those Bribes Abroad," *Fortune*, July 1976, p. 180.

4. *Ibid.*

5. This case occurred before the 1977 Foreign Corrupt Practices Act.

6. Lawrence Kohlberg, *The Psychology of Moral Development*. (New York: Harper & Row, 1984), p. 640.

7. Lawrence Kohlberg, *The Philosophy of Moral Development*. (New York: Harper & Row, 1981), p. 121.

8. *Ibid.*

9. It is theoretically possible to have a different principle, like utility, as the highest principle. For a philosophical account of why the principle of respect is superior to utility as the highest principle, see Alan Donagan, *The Theory of Morality*, (Chicago: University of Chicago Press, 1977), chapter 6.

10. Viewed from the perspective of positive law, this is a case of stealing. However, at the post-conventional level, it is not morally a case of wrongful taking, given the conditions that we have described. This is consonant with the traditional scholastic distinction between taking and theft. For example, see Thomas Aquinas, *Summa Theologiae*, II-II, 66, 7.

11. Our definition of a professional is normative. Sociological descriptions of people may show that people who call themselves professionals do not always act according to Level Three. But that shows a problem with their actions, not with our definition. We disagree with Michael Bayles's view that the definition of professionalism must be merely descriptive. See his *Professional Ethics* (Belmont, CA: Wadsworth, 1981), pp. 7-11. After all, the term is often used with a strong normative content as when someone says, "That person's actions aren't very professional." Our definition is essentially similar to the idea of *techné* as explained in Plato's *Gorgias*. Following the classical distinction between a craft and a knack, virtually any activity could be done professionally. An exception might be a "hit-man," for example.

Something that we normally consider a professional activity could be done unprofessionally. A surgeon may simply have a knack. In some contexts, the concept of a professional may include other characteristics as well.

12. See Appendix 1 for examples of codes of ethics.

13. Allan Bloom, *The Closing of the American Mind.* (New York: Touchstone Books, 1988).

14. *Business Week*, August 29, 1988. p. 36.

15. We recognize that such cases are complicated since some doctors participate in physician-owned facilities because they can be better suited to provide prompt and efficient services. Some doctors also contend that ownership gives them more control over maintaining quality. The problem may be not only an individual moral problem, but a systemic one.

16. "A Conversation with John Noonan," *U.S. News and World Report*, July 8, 1985, p. 64.

17. *Ibid.*

Chapter 3

Rules and Relationships

What is the basis of ethics: rules or relationships?

In light of Chapter Two, you may get the impression that ethics is primarily a matter of rules. After all, we have just shown how what seems to be a rule, the principle of respect, can provide order to moral dilemmas faced by professionals. So you may have the impression that ethics means following rules.

However, it is important to realize that the ethical life is not simply a matter of rule-following for its own sake. The principle of respect for persons entails more than empty, abstract rules. The ethical life, where the primary emphasis is on respect for persons, includes caring for people, acting with concern for the welfare of others, entering into relationships of trust, and developing character traits that foster such relationships. Someone that follows rules without genuine care and concern for others does not really treat persons with respect. Living ethically means living according to the spirit of the law, not just the letter of the law. Therefore, the ethical life is more than mere rule-following.

Gilligan's Critique of Kohlberg's Theory

Carol Gilligan has been critical of Kohlberg's approach, claiming that he puts too much emphasis on moral rules, and not enough accent on relationships. While she was a research psychologist with Kohlberg at Harvard, she noticed that girls tended to score lower than boys when tested using Kohlberg's scale of moral development. She claimed that

Kohlberg's method of evaluating moral development emphasized rules and was therefore biased against females. This led Gilligan to search for a different model of moral development, one that takes into account female moral development. This model emphasizes care and relationships, rather than abstract rules.

In her studies, Gilligan noted that there is a difference in moral development between boys and girls from early childhood. She draws on the work of the psychologist Jean Piaget. He found that as boys mature, they gain an increasing interest in "the legal elaboration of rules and the development of fair procedures for adjudicating conflicts, a fascination that, he notes, does not hold for girls."[1] Gilligan finds further support in the work of the psychologist Janet Lever. She studied elementary school children, aged ten and eleven, watching them during play. Recording her observations, she reported a number of differences in the way boys play as compared to girls. Gilligan summarizes her findings:

> Boys play out of doors more often than girls do; boys play more often in large and age-heterogeneous groups; they play competitive games more often, and their games last longer than girls' games. The last is in some ways the most interesting finding. Boys' games appeared to last longer not only because they required a higher level of skill and were thus less likely to become boring, but also because, when disputes arose in the course of a game, boys were able to resolve the disputes more effectively than girls: "During the course of this study, boys were seen quarreling all the time, but not once was a game terminated because of a quarrel and no game was interrupted for more than seven minutes. In the gravest debates, the final word was always, to 'repeat the play,' generally followed by a chorus of 'cheater's proof.'" In fact, it seemed that the boys enjoyed the legal debates as much as they did the game itself, and even marginal players of lesser size or skill participated equally in these recurrent squabbles. In contrast, the eruption of disputes among girls tended to end the game.[2]

According to Gilligan, the bias toward male development arises from an assumption that the male model, with its emphasis on rules, is better suited to "fit the requirements for modern corporate success. In contrast, the sensitivity and care for the feelings of others that girls develop through their play have little market value and can even impede professional success."[3] The implication is that if young girls want to succeed professionally, they need to learn to play like boys. In other words, the man's world is one where you have to play by the rules, and even learn to "play" the rules. So, Gilligan is critical of a rule-based ethic, pointing out that it can disregard the significance of human care and relationships in the moral life.[4]

In contrast with the legalistic attitude exhibited in boys' play, the games girls play do not promote opportunities for confrontation and conflict resolution.

> Traditional girls' games like jump rope and hopscotch are turn-taking games, where competition is indirect since one person's success does not necessarily signify another's failure. Consequently, disputes requiring adjudication are less likely to occur. In fact, most of the girls whom Lever interviewed claimed that when a quarrel broke out, they ended the game. Rather than elaborating a system of rules for resolving disputes, girls subordinated the continuation of the game to the continuation of relationships.[5]

The inference that Gilligan draws from this is that the moral development of females is different from that of males. Females focus on relationships. Males focus on rules.

Gilligan and an Ethic of Caring

Gilligan found that females tended to score lower on Kohlberg's evaluations of moral development because the tests themselves were biased to favor males. Boys, who tended to solve the Heinz dilemma by focusing on the rules of property and individual rights, scored higher than girls, who tended to focus on the relationship between Heinz and his wife. Gilligan suggests that the orientation of females tends to focus on relationships, social context and interconnectedness rather than rules, autonomy and individualism. She calls this orientation the care ethic.

Gilligan has pointed to a dimension of the moral life that tends to be overlooked and undervalued in much of modern ethical thought. With the rise of modern science in the seventeenth and eighteenth centuries, moral theory began to emphasize individuality and rational, procedural rules. Just as scientists sought to understand the natural world by breaking it down into its atomic elements, moral theorists of the enlightenment tended to understand the moral life by breaking down human actions so that they can be studied as individual, autonomous elements. This has led to the modern moral emphasis on individual rights, at the expense of communal bonds.

The traditional ethical insights of Classical Greek, Roman and Medieval culture, as well as Biblical culture, place communal bonds at the center of the ethical life. Whether it is the notion of the *polis* in Ancient Greece, of civic responsibility and hospitality in Ancient Rome, of chivalry and civil manners in medieval culture, or of love of neighbor in Biblical culture, each place a high emphasis on acting with care in human relationships.

The modern enlightenment movement, with its emphasis on individuality and autonomy, was a reaction against social privileges that were embedded in traditional communal bonds. There was a positive development that arose out of the enlightenment emphasis on individuality, since it stressed equality. However, in the process of emphasizing equal human rights, modern morality lost sight of communal responsibility and the notion of care and concern that older moral traditions recognized.[6]

Gilligan's criticism of Kohlberg's emphasis on rules can be seen as a positive contribution to moral theory since it helps us to recover several key elements of the moral life.

The Limits of an Ethic of Caring

Gilligan has provided a helpful criticism of an ethical approach that is based on abstract rules. The ethic of caring that she promotes is an attempt to counter what she sees as an unhealthy ethic of rules. While we agree with Gilligan that relationships are an important element in the moral life, an overemphasis on relationships is also potentially unhealthy. Not all relationships contribute to human well-being. An ethic that blindly focuses on caring and maintaining human relationships cannot by itself distinguish between relationship-maintaining and relationship-promoting actions. That is, a relationship-maintaining ethic would avoid conflict in order to maintain the relationship, whether the relationship was healthy or not.

Recent studies on co-dependency have detailed ways in which people, very often women, maintain unhealthy relationships such as those entailing abuse or alcohol and chemical dependence.[7] The moral challenge that such women face is not that they need to learn to care - sometimes they seem to care too much.[8] For example, spouses and children of alcoholics often develop a pattern of response that maintains the unhealthy behavior rather than risking a break in the relationship.

With the introduction of the principle of respect, we can distinguish between healthy and unhealthy relationships. The principle of respect for persons is a criterion for promoting healthy relationships. Acting in accord with the principle of respect will entail not only relationship-maintaining actions, but also actions that challenge unhealthy relationships. In this way, conflict can sometimes be valuable.

Therefore, Gilligan's approach is limited since it lacks any critical test for relationships. Principles and relationships are interdependent aspects of the moral life. Moral principles should express what is embodied in healthy human relationships.

Problems with Rules and Relationships

So far, we have shown that an ethic that is based solely on rules has a problem. As Gilligan has pointed out, there is an important aspect to the moral life that is not reducible to rules. An ethic that focuses exclusively on rules is so abstract that it can become an ethic without care. The moral life is not a matter of rule-worship.

Without the care and concern that Gilligan describes, those with the rule-worshipping mentality may ultimately lose the ability to follow moral rules. As soon as a person learns how to "play" the rules, they begin to manipulate rules for their own purposes. This is the attitude that we have seen played out in some recent Wall Street scandals, or in the Savings and Loan crisis where bankers unscrupulously gutted banks, often manipulating the rules in place for their own material gain.

But just as an ethic of rules is problematic, so is an ethic of relationships. Relationships without rules are blind. An ethic of care that is not guided by sound moral principles cannot distinguish between healthy and unhealthy relationships.

A Complete Ethic is Not Gender Specific

Gilligan has provided some important insights into the moral life insofar as she has reminded us of the importance of care and human relationships in the moral life. However, she goes too far when she suggests that women have a different kind of moral reasoning than men, an ethic of caring.

The principle of respect for persons, which is the central idea in Kohlberg's model, need not exclude the idea of caring. A complete ethic should include both the idea of acting according to principle and with care. In fact, late in his career, Kohlberg acknowledged that the responsibility orientation suggested by Gilligan's studies augments his own approach. In response to Gilligan, Kohlberg claimed that his research led him to hypothesize that most actions involve two judgmental aspects:

> a deontic judgment of rights and duties and a second judgment of personal responsibility for action in the situation. The usefulness of Gilligan's ideas in casting light on puzzles in our own data was a major opening for us, and we adapted her concept of "responsibility" to mediate between both male and female judgment and action: we saw judgments of responsibility as activating "follow through" from deontic judgment to action.[9]

In other words, justice tells us what is right; responsibility moves us to carry it out. There is not, therefore, a different ethic for men and women. Ethically mature human beings should act with respect, living up to the demands of justice and acting with responsibility, thus promoting healthy human relationships.

Rules and Principles

A rule is a Level Two standard for decision-making. It proscribes or prescribes certain actions, for example, "Do not kill," "Do not steal," "Love your neighbor."[10] Rules gain their force from social convention or agreement. They are often a handy guide for making decisions in everyday situations. But an ethic based solely on rules has certain problems, including these four. 1) An ethic of rules can tend toward rigid legalism. 2) People can learn to "play" the rules, twisting them to their own advantage. 3) Rules usually work in normal situations, but they do not provide a principled way to solve moral dilemmas. In the Heinz dilemma, there are two rules that collide: do not steal and provide for your family. 4) The society may be so corrupt that it promotes bad rules. For example, in some societies, the social norm is to give and take bribes. Following the socially expected moral rules of that culture, or any culture, is unprincipled. While rules have a place in the moral life, something more is needed.

A moral principle is "a method of making a choice, a way of perceiving and selecting moral components of a situation, a specification of the moral point of view."[11] In other words, a moral principle is an objective guide to choosing actions that promote healthy human relationships. It derives its moral force from its concern for human dignity. In Chapter Four, we list seven moral principles. These serve as general guides, providing a basic framework for determining whether an action is morally permissible, impermissible or obligatory. With regard to the Heinz dilemma, a decision based on moral principle is responsive to both the generality of this class of situations and sensitive to the uniqueness of the particular circumstances of the case.

How does Gilligan's emphasis on relationships fit in? It is evident that though an ethic of caring may be incompatible with an ethic of rules, it is not necessarily incompatible with an ethic of principles. Gilligan's concern for responsibility provides the link between abstract principles and concrete action.

Conclusion

We think that Kohlberg's model can provide a complete ethic and an adequate guide to the moral life for professionals. From a feminist perspective, Gilligan has shown us that there may be a propensity in males to focus on rules and disregard relationships. Nonetheless, an ethic of caring that is devoid of moral principle is as problematic as an ethic of rules that is devoid of care. A complete ethic is one based on respect for persons, an ethic that includes care and acting according to principle. Moral principles are used to guide actions that promote healthy human relationships. In professional life, following the model we are proposing, there is a place for principles and caring, for rules and relationships, for interests and roles.

Questions for Review and Discussion

1. Give an example of a rule that disregards healthy human relationships.

2. Give an example of a relationship that fails to promote human dignity.

3. Do you think that there is a different ethic for men and women?

4. What is the difference between a rule and a principle?

5. Can we gain a better understanding of the moral life by looking at patterns of moral development in males and females?

Notes to Chapter Three

1. Carol Gilligan, *In Another Voice: Psychological Theory and Women's Development*. (Cambridge: Harvard University Press, 1982), p. 10.

2. *Ibid.*, p. 9.

3. *Ibid.*, p. 10.

4. It is not clear whether Gilligan thinks that males should adopt an ethic of caring, or whether there are two equally valid ethics, a masculine ethic of rules and a feminine ethic of caring. Some feminists have used Gilligan's approach to argue that an ethic of caring is superior, and have thereby been critical of the current corporate model.

5. Gilligan, p. 10.

6. Robert Nisbet has developed this theme in *The Social Philosophers*.

7. For example, see Melody Beattie, *CoDependent No More: How to Stop Controlling Others and Start Caring for Yourself*. (New York: HarperCollins, 1987).

8. Robin Norwood, *Women Who Love Too Much: A Closer Look at Relationship Addiction and Recovery*. (Los Angeles: Jeremy P. Tarcher, Inc. 1986).

9. Lawrence Kohlberg, "A Reply to Owen Flanagan and Some Comments on the Puka-Goodpaster Exchange," *Ethics* (92) 1982: 514.

10. We follow Kohlberg, who follows Richard Hare, on the distinction between a moral rule and a moral principle. See Lawrence Kohlberg, "A Reply to Owen Flanagan and Some Comments on the Puka-Goodpaster Exchange," *Ethics* (92) 1982: 520.

11. *Ibid.*

Chapter 4

Moral Principles

Since you will face many difficult moral decisions as a professional, it will be helpful for you to become familiar with several moral principles to guide your actions. The seven principles that we set forth in this chapter will help you cut through the complexity and confusion of the moral problems you will encounter.

Although we set out seven principles, it is important to understand that they are all derived from one basic, fundamental principle: respect for persons. Therefore, they are all consistent with the basic principle of respect, provided that they are considered in the order that we present them. There is a hierarchy of importance to these principles.

We intend that these principles be applied from the perspective of the third level of moral judgment in Kohlberg's model, the level of post-conventional reasoning.[1] The basic idea that informs the highest level of moral judgment is the notion of respect for persons. This idea often comes in a moment of moral insight. The individual who has this insight sees that it is not just people in one's own group or society that have moral worth, but that all human beings have a basic dignity that is worthy of respect. Someone who has had this moral insight, and chosen to live according to this insight, makes moral decisions as a member of a universal moral community.

The most basic, fundamental moral principle from this perspective is:

THE PRINCIPLE OF RESPECT

In every action and every intention, in every goal and every means, treat every human being, yourself and others, with the respect befitting the dignity and worth of a person.

The main concept in the principle of respect is the idea that every human being has inherent dignity and worth. The worth of human beings differs from that of objects that we use. Things have exchange value. They are replaceable. Human beings, on the other hand, have infinite worth because as subjects capable of choice they are unique and therefore irreplaceable.

The respect referred to in this principle is not the same thing that is meant when someone says "I really respect that person," or "You have to earn my respect." These are special kinds of respect that are similar to admiration. The principle of respect entails a general respect due to all persons.

Since human beings are free in the sense that they are capable of making choices, human beings should be treated as ends, and not as means only.[2] In other words, human beings should not be used and treated like objects. Things may be manipulated and used, but a subject's ability to choose must be respected.

One easy criterion that can be used to determine if you are treating someone with respect is to consider whether your action is reversible. In other words, would you want someone to do the same thing to you that you are about to do to them? This is the basic idea involved in the Golden Rule: "Do unto others as you would have them do unto you." But the idea is not unique to Christianity. Over one hundred years before the birth of Christ, a pagan asked Rabbi Hillel to explain the entire law of Moses while standing on one foot. Hillel summed up the massive body of Jewish law by raising one foot and saying, "Do not do to others what you would hate for them to do to you."[3]

The idea of respect is a rich concept. It contains the essence of what the moral life is about. The idea is so broad, however, that it is sometimes difficult to know how it applies in particular cases. It is helpful, therefore, to derive other less basic principles from the principle of respect.

It is worth noting that in applied ethics, the more concrete the case is, the more places there are where controversy can enter in. The greatest difficulty in this area is applying an abstract principle to the particularities of a given case. Therefore, more specific expressions of the general principle of respect are helpful. Two such principles are the principle of non-malevolence and the principle of benevolence.

THE PRINCIPLE OF NON-MALEVOLENCE

In all of your actions, avoid harming people.

Resect for persons requires that one does not intend to harm others. Intentional harm is morally impermissible, because it fails to recognize the inherent worth of persons as subjects.

Beyond the basic requirement not to intentionally harm, non-malevolence entails a number of slightly more subtle ideas relating to unintentional harm. A person who acts negligently, even though they may have a good intention, can do harm that violates the principle of respect. There are two different kinds of negligence. One stems from ignorance of fact and the other from ignorance of principle.

Negligence that stems from ignorance of fact is incompetence. As a professional with special skills and knowledge, you will be expected to be knowledgeable in your area of expertise. In addition to your original training, this includes keeping current. Further, professionals are obliged to know the relevant details of the cases that they are working on. In the Paul Newman film "The Verdict," a physician was negligent in that he was ignorant of a particular fact. He administered anaesthesia to a woman and overlooked her medical chart that showed she had eaten an hour before. As a result, the woman was permanently incapacitated. In this case, the physician did not know something he should have known, causing harm to his patient.

Another kind of negligence stems from ignorance of moral principles. As a professional, you are expected to know the moral ramifications of your craft. This includes cases of insensitivity as well as of willfully ignoring the moral obligations of one's profession. There is a common attitude that the moral life can prohibit you from "getting the job done." In this setting, you might be tempted to ignore your moral obligations. Because this kind of ignorance can cause harm, it is a form of negligence.

Another principle that follows from the principle of respect for persons is the principle of benevolence.

THE PRINCIPLE OF BENEVOLENCE

Promote the well-being of others.

The principle of benevolence requires more action than the principle of non-malevolence. As long as you passively mind your own business, you are probably following the principle of non-malevolence. But the principle of benevolence recognizes that respecting people sometimes implies actively responding to their needs.

The principle of benevolence applies especially in relation to those who are unable to help themselves. For example, suppose that you are driving your car down a rural road and you see another car that has been in an accident. You stop and find that the driver is injured and unconscious. The principle of non-malevolence would require that you avoid harming the person more, by, say, stealing their wallet! So by minding your own business and just driving away, you would be satisfying the principle of non-malevolence. But the principle of benevolence requires caring action, and doing more than just minding your own business.

The caring action required by the principle of benevolence would in this case require that if you can do something to help the injured person, then you are morally obligated to do so. However, if you lack the specialized knowledge or training required to provide help, then you should at least seek aid from someone who can help. In other words, ought implies can. That is, you are obliged to help insofar as you are able.

When this is applied to professional life, it means that you have a duty to promote the welfare of others with your specialized skill and training. When your expertise can be used for human good, it should be. When you are faced with a case demanding skills beyond your own expertise, you should seek appropriate help or refer the case to someone suited to help. In this way, professionalism implies cooperation with others who have specialized skills and training.

The principle of benevolence does not imply that you should be a busy body. Just because you should work to promote the well-being of others, it does not follow that you should ignore the autonomy of others by making their decisions for them. Human well-being includes being able to make independent choices.

Still, there are times when it is appropriate to "butt in," especially when someone is clearly unable to care for themselves. Respect for others implies that we promote the well-being of children, orphans, the grieving, the injured, and in general those unable to care for themselves. This involves working to help them become able to care for themselves and others.

The principle of respect applies not only to others, but also to oneself. For a professional, respecting yourself means acting with integrity.

THE PRINCIPLE OF INTEGRITY

Maintain personal standards of conduct befitting a professional; respect yourself in all of your decisions so as to be worthy of living a fulfilling professional life.

As a professional, respecting yourself means acting consistently. The basic idea in integrity is that a personal commitment to a moral life allows you to hold together the many particular actions that make up your life.

The idea of integrity is shown in a story told by Socrates.[4] Suppose there was a magic ring that would make you invisible as long as you were wearing it. How would you act while you were invisible? A person of integrity would continue to act based on the principle of respect for persons whether they had the magic ring on or not, whether or not they were being watched by others. Professionals with integrity do not need a watchdog group constantly monitoring their behavior.

A special aspect of professional integrity involves basing your actions on professional competence. This includes two things. First, you should acquire and maintain the technical skills and knowledge necessary to carry out your professional duties. Second, you should know the limits of your knowledge and skills and not transgress those limits, either through negligence or fakery. So when the principle of respect gets applied to the individual dimensions of professional life, it is expressed in the ideal of integrity.

THE PRINCIPLE OF JUSTICE

Treat others in a manner that is appropriate to them as human beings; be fair, treating people equally, i.e., in similar ways in similar circumstances.

The main idea in the principle of justice is treating people appropriately. This idea can be expressed in a number of different ways, since there are a number of different aspects to justice. These include substantive, distributive, commutative, procedural, and retributive justice.

1. Substantive Justice.

Substantive justice is an ideal principle governing social relations. As an ideal, this principle functions as a goal of social organization. It is the aspiration of achieving a society where people live in right relation with one another. This is the ideal of justice that was held by one of the original American settlers, John Winthrop (1588-1649). While governor of the Massachusetts Bay Colony, Winthrop caught a man stealing firewood from his woodpile during a severe winter. Reasoning from the perspective of substantive justice, Winthrop

> called the man into his presence and told him that because of the severity of the winter and his need, he had permission to supply himself from Winthrop's woodpile for the rest of the cold season. Thus, he said to his friends, did he effectively cure the man from stealing.[5]

Winthrop considered the act to be just. The end result was more important than following the letter of the law. In this way, substantive justice focuses on the end result, the goal of promoting a healthy community.

2. Distributive Justice.

Distributive justice is a principle governing the distribution of social and material goods. It recognizes that basic human needs ought to be met (insofar as they can be met), and that similar needs have an equal claim. Distributive justice is concerned with providing a proper share of essential goods to each person.

When evaluating what constitutes a proper share, one should remember the difference between equality of opportunity and equality of condition. Equality of opportunity states that everyone should have a fair chance at acquiring basic goods. Equality of condition is the state where everyone has the same amount of goods. Distributive justice does not necessarily demand equality of condition, though it does demand equality of opportunity.

3. Commutative Justice.

Commutative justice entails the idea of unbiased fairness. It includes the notion of reversibility. Following commutative justice, people could change places, and still agree to the essential fairness of the action. John Rawls developed a notion of justice using the idea of a veil of ignorance.[6] Behind this veil, no one knows their place in life. An action is fair if everyone would agree to it while they are behind the veil. Commutative justice implies that similar cases deserve similar treatment.

4. Procedural Justice.

Procedural justice is concerned with establishing fair means of administration. It is especially concerned with the fair and consistent application of rules, policies and laws. By itself, procedural justice is incomplete, since the fair and consistent application of rules cannot guarantee fair results. Procedural justice is a means, though by itself it does not provide any goal. Laws may be applied fairly, but that does not guarantee that the content of the laws is just. Justice requires that the procedures that we establish to attain a goal should be consistent with the goal. In other words, the end does not justify the means. Unjust procedural means cannot attain the goal of substantive justice.

Procedural justice complements substantive justice. Substantive justice provides a vision of the goal that justice strives towards. Procedural justice is concerned with consistency and fairness in applying laws to achieve that goal. Both are needed, since one without the other is inadequate.

5. Retributive Justice.

Retributive justice entails giving people their due. Though the idea of retribution is often associated with punishment, it is not restricted to the notion that people should be punished for bad actions, since it also implies that good actions should be rewarded. This aspect of justice stems from the recognition that choices have consequences. Therefore, it is appropriate to fairly reward and punish actions according to their merit. This is an important moral concept in the legal profession, though the question of fair rewards and punishments is applicable in many professional situations.

All of these aspects of justice are supposed to express a single unified idea of justice. These different aspects should be consistent with one another. However, it is possible to overemphasize one at the expense of another. Vigilantes who break the law in order to bring about justice may be overemphasizing substantive justice while ignoring procedural justice. On the other hand, procedural justice in itself may not be identical with substantive justice. A blind obedience to procedural rules may not be in conformity with the principle of respect, since strict, impersonal adherence to procedures may lead to treating persons as objects. So when the principle of respect gets applied to the social dimensions of professional life, it is expressed in the ideal of justice.

THE PRINCIPLE OF UTILITY

Given that the intention and the goal of your action treat people with respect, choose the course of action that produces the greatest benefit for the greatest number of people.

The emphasis of this principle is on the consequences of the action. It assumes however that you have acted out of a respect for persons. If you have a choice between two morally permissible actions, choose the one that has the best outcome for the most people.

Some moralists have overemphasized the consequences of action, claiming that utility is the fundamental principle of moral judgment. Thinkers like Jeremy Bentham and John Stuart Mill have developed entire moral theories based on the concept of utility. For them, an action is judged by the bottom line, not by the intention.[7]

However, there are two problems with overemphasizing utility. First, by disregarding motive and intention, utilitarian thinkers miss an important aspect of the moral life. The intention of the act defines what the act is. The intention is the belief that explains the act. For example, to understand what a vaccination is, you must focus on the intention. The behavior of injecting a person appears the same whether the intention is to vaccinate or sadistically cause pain. If a medical professional injects a patient with the intention of causing them pain, the action is morally wrong because they have violated the principle of respect and especially the principle of non-malevolence. Even if the injection ends up resulting in a cure, the bad intention makes it a bad act. On the other hand, if a medical professional injects a patient with the intention of curing that patient using an accepted procedure, even if it causes pain and does not produce the desired result, the action is good. The intention of treating people with respect is of primary importance.

The second problem with overemphasizing consequences is that it assumes you can accurately predict the outcome of every action. We have all had the experience of trying to bring about some result and failing through no fault of our own. On the other hand, we have all also had the experience of bringing about a desired result unintentionally or by accident.

For example, imagine a thief who holds up a store, threatening to shoot the clerk. Unbeknownst to the thief, the clerk has had the hiccoughs for over a year. The thief pulls the trigger, but his gun misfires. As a result, the clerk's hiccoughs are cured! If results alone determine the moral worth of an action, then this was a morally good act.[8]

Utility is a principle of action that is prominent in many professional activities like business, engineering and medicine. Efficiency is a significant consideration, but it is sometimes overemphasized, so that the only thing viewed to be important is "getting the job done." But if the consequences are not placed in their proper place in a hierarchy, then considerations of utility often conflict with respect for persons as individuals. For example, in the 1970's, Ford Motor company used a strictly utilitarian mode of thinking in determining whether to add an $11 rubber bladder to protect the gas tank on the Ford Pinto. Using a cost/benefit analysis, they determined that it would cost $137 million to add the part, and only $49.5 million to pay out benefits to those killed and injured in accidents resulting from erupting gas tanks. By focusing solely on the consequences through their cost/benefit analysis model, a consideration of respect for their consumers as individuals was neglected.

The results are important. Treating people with respect involves being concerned for their welfare and doing actions that benefit people. However, the consequences are not the most important element in the moral life. The primary principle is to treat people with respect. Consequences are important, though not primary.

THE PRINCIPLE OF DOUBLE EFFECT

Given that the intention and goal of your action treat people with respect, make sure that there are no foreseeable bad side effects that are disproportionate with the good of the main effect.

Actions usually have more than one consequence. A good action may have a double effect. If you walk to the store while it is raining, you intend to go to the store, but you foresee that you will get wet. If you get a vaccination, you intend that the medication will bring health, but you foresee that the shot will be painful. In both of these cases, the bad consequence is foreseeable, and it is necessarily linked with the good, but the bad side effect is unintended. Since the intention is primarily what gives an action its moral worth, the acts are not bad, even though they produce bad effects.[9]

However, sometimes the foreseeable consequences of an action are so serious that they may outweigh the good intention. For example, suppose that you want to manufacture a product that is needed in the local economy. Your intention is good. But in order to build a manufacturing plant, it is necessary to clear 200 acres of land and drain a wetland reserve. This will entail radically altering the environment and thus endangering a certain rare species that is critical to the stable functioning of the local habitat and ecosystem. Even though the intention is good, that does not completely settle the question as to whether it is a good act. If the bad consequence outweighs the good intended effect, then the principle of double effect prohibits the action. The principle of double effect serves to limit unintended harm. In this way, the intention of the action is the primary concern, but it is not the only concern.

The principle of double effect helps us to decide when we may permit the existence of a bad side effect that accompanies a good action. There are four conditions that guide in the application of the principle of double effect.

1. The intention must be morally permissible.

2. Distinguish between the good intended effect and the undesirable foreseeable side effect.

3. The bad side effect must not be intended for itself.

4. The good of the intended effect must be proportionate with the bad of the foreseeable effect.

These four conditions apply, for example, in the case of self-defense. Suppose a police officer is called in regarding a domestic dispute. Upon arrival, the officer finds the couple arguing, and the man holding a butcher knife. The man turns to the officer and begins to attack with the knife. In such a case, is it permissible to use lethal force in self-defense?

1. The intention of defending oneself is good.

2. The good intended effect is the defense of one's life. The undesirable side effect is injury to the attacker, even perhaps lethal injury.

3. The officer's intention must not be to harm the attacker, even though harm is foreseen.

4. The good of saving one's life is proportionate with the harm inflicted.

Therefore, in some cases, the principle of double effect can be used to permit the existence of some bad side effects within clear limits.

Suppose an accountant misappropriates funds in order to help pay her mother's medical bills. The principle of double effect would show that this action is morally impermissible, since the first condition is not met. Or suppose a police officer arrests someone who is carrying a weapon. The officer not only uses a club to knock the weapon away, but beats the person even after the threat of harm has been eliminated. Such an action is morally impermissible, for the third condition has not been met. Finally, consider a case where a businessperson orders the pilot of his private plane to fly through dangerous weather to complete a business deal that will only net a small profit.[10] In this case, the fourth condition would require considering whether the foreseeable danger is disproportionate with the intended outcome.

The principle of double effect is somewhat unique, because it does not apply in every case. It only applies when a bad effect is unavoidably connected with a good intention. In those cases, the four conditions outlined above can be used to help in moral decision-making.

Conclusion

These seven principles provide a basic framework for determining whether an action is morally permissible, impermissible or obligatory. If you keep in mind the hierarchy of importance to these principles, you can be reasonably sure that with prudent application, you will make sound moral decisions.

Diagram 2

Moral Principles

THE PRINCIPLE OF RESPECT

In every action and every intention, in every goal and every means, treat every human beingh, yourself and others, with the respect befitting the dignity and worth of a person.

THE PRINCIPLE OF NON-MALEVOLENCE

In all of your actions, avoid harming people.

THE PRINCIPLE OF BENEVOLENCE

Promote the well being of others.

THE PRINCIPLE OF INTEGRITY

Maintain personal standards of conduct befitting a professional; respect yourself in all of your decisions so as to be worthy of living a fulfilling professional life.

THE PRINCIPLE OF JUSTICE

Treat others in a manner that is appropriate to them as human beings; be fair, treating people equally, i.e., in similar ways in similar circumstances.

THE PRINCIPLE OF UTILITY

Given that the intention and the goal of your action treat people with respect, choose the course of action that produces the greatest benefit for the greatest number of people.

THE PRINCIPLE OF DOUBLE EFFECT

Given that the intention and goal of your action treat people with respect, make sure that there are no foreseeable bad side effects that are disproportionate with the good of the main effect.

Questions for Review and Discussion

1. Explain the relationship between the principle of respect and the other moral principles.

2. Explain the difference between principles that require action and those that prohibit action.

3. Explain the difference between duties to yourself, duties to others, and duties that apply to both yourself and others.

4. Do you think that the consequences of an action ever outweigh the respect due an individual?

5. Describe a situation in which the principle of double effect would apply. How is that different from a case of intentionally doing something morally wrong to produce a good result?

Notes to Chapter Four

1. We understand that not everyone studying professional ethics will have matured to the highest level of moral judgment. Further, there is a tendency for those at the lower levels to try to interpret post-conventional principles in terms of self-interest or social convention. Our hope is that by encouraging professionals and pre-professionals to think in terms of the most mature level of moral judgment, their moral development will be aided.

2. Immanuel Kant, *Foundation of the Metaphysics of Morals*. Trans. Lewis White Beck. (New York: Library of Liberal Arts, 1959). Kant's formulation of the categorical imperative, that is, the fundamental principle of ethics, is "Act so that you treat humanity, whether in you own person, or in that of another, always as an end and never as a means only." p. 47.

3. There are several sophisticated and perhaps subtle problems with the Golden Rule as it relates to the principle of respect. See Alan Donagan, *The Theory of Morality*, (Chicago: University of Chicago Press, 1977), chapter 2.

4. Plato, *Republic*, Book 2, 359d ff.

5. Robert Bellah, et. al., *Habits of the Heart*, p. 29.

6. John Rawls, *A Theory of Justice*. (Cambridge: Harvard University Press, 1971).

7. The classic expression of utilitarian ethics is John Stuart Mill's *Utilitarianism*, first published in 1863.

8. This example was used in an article by Greg Beabout titled "Morphine Use for Terminal Cancer Patients: An Application of the Principle of Double Effect," *Philosophy in Context*, Vol. 19, 1989, p. 49.

9. In the 19th century, J.P. Gury stated a widely held version of the principle of double effect. See J.P. Gury, S.J., *Compendium Theologiae Moralis*, 5th ed. (Ratisbon, 1874), vol. 1, tr. *de actibus humanis*, c. 2, n. 9. Given the distinction between intention and cause that we describe in Chapter Five, we reject Gury's account of double effect which tends to reduce intentions to causes. Instead, our version is closer to Grisez's as presented in Donagan's *The Theory of Morality*.

10. This example is used in *Fagothey's Right and Reason*, Revised by Milton A. Gonsalves, 8th Edition, (Columbus: Merrill, 1986), p. 45.

Chapter 5

Applying Moral Principles: Intention, Motive, Circumstance

The most difficult aspect of ethics is applying moral principles to actual cases. In Chapter Four, we described seven basic moral principles. In this chapter, we will discuss how those principles can be applied. This involves looking at three things: first the intention, then the motive, and finally the circumstances.

There are two challenges in applying ethics. The first is to make good decisions based upon sound ethical principles. Ethics is not just a theoretical, abstract activity. In each particular case you have to know what to do. How do the principles apply in different situations? The second challenge is to act on your decision. Once you have a moral understanding of the situation and the special circumstances surrounding it, you have to have the character to do what is right.

As Carol Gilligan has noted, an overemphasis on moral rules can lead to rigid legalism.[1] The moral life is more than a set of abstract rules. Living well entails being able to prudently apply sound moral principles to the particular circumstances of each concrete case. How do you do this?

The Need for an Accurate Description of the Act

In order to know if an act is morally good, you have to have an accurate description of the act. This will involve separating out the intention, the motive and the circumstances of the act. Moral confusion arises in applied ethics when these elements are not clearly distinguished.

For a moral evaluation, an accurate description of the act must focus on the intention of the act. The intention of the action is the belief that explains the action. A behavioral description of the physical events of an action would be inadequate for a moral assessment.

Suppose you see a woman point her left arm out the driver's side window of a car. A clinical, behavioral description of the act would be "she raised her arm to the open window and then stretched it out to the left." For a moral assessment, it is necessary to know the intention. In fact, it is not possible to know what the action is without a primary emphasis on the intention. The outstretched arm could be a signal that she is going to turn left, though it could be that the driver is pointing at someone or even swatting at a fly. What the act is depends on the driver's intention.

Consider this behavioral description of an act. A man squeezes his index finger on the trigger of a gun. Without a description of the intention, it is impossible to know whether this is an act of demonstrating how the gun works, of cleaning the gun, or of murder. Or consider a case of someone injecting a hypodermic needle into someone's arm. It is only when we focus on the intention that we can accurately describe the act. For example, the injection could be either a vaccination or a poisoning.

Therefore, what the action is cannot be reduced to what is observed. In addition to the overt observable act, an accurate description must include the intention, that is, the belief that explains the act.

In recent discussions of this issue, contemporary philosophers have debated whether the intention of an action can be reduced to a cause of the action, whether the cause is observable or not. Most notably, Donald Davidson has argued that just as all natural events have a cause, all actions have a cause, which is the intention.[2] Davidson has an example which runs as follows.

> I flip the switch, turn on the light, and illuminate the room. Unbeknownst to me I also alert a prowler to the fact that I am home. Here I do not do four things, but only one, of which four descriptions have been given.[3]

However, several thinkers have challenged Davidson's claim that intentions are causes. Joseph Margolis, one of Davidson's critics, claims that Davidson cannot hold both that intentions are causes and that the above example contains four different descriptions of one action.

> It seems plain that a man may intend to flip the switch without intending to turn on the light or without intending to illuminate the room. . . . But if this is so, then intentions for particular actions are description-relative: one can have an intention for an action under one description without having a relevant intention for the very same action under another description. But if this is the case, then having an intention is not as such a cause of an action, if causes, as we seem to hold, are not description-relative.[4]

Margolis' argument is that if intentions are causes, and turning on the light is the very same action as alerting the burglar, and I wanted to turn on the light, then I must have wanted to alert the burglar. Turning on the light is the very same action as alerting the burglar and I wanted to turn on the light, but I did not want to alert the burglar. Therefore, intentions are different than causes because intentions are description-relative while causes are not.

Another philosopher, Richard Taylor, makes a similar point with a different example. He writes:

> Compare the following three situations: (i) a man raises his hand in order to attract the speaker's attention, and thereby both attracts the speaker's attention and drives off a fly; (ii) he raises his hand in the same way in order to attract the chairman's attention, and thereby attracts the speaker's attention and drives off a fly; (iii) he raises his hand in the same way in order to drive off a fly, and thereby attracts the speaker's attention and drives off a fly. Now exactly the same things happen in each situation. The effects that actually occur are all the same, though not all these effects are the ends or purposes of the man's action in each case. . . . The differences in the three situations are not, then, differences of causes or effects, whether these be of the observable or unobservable kind, but simply and solely differences of means and ends.[5]

In each example, the intention is different, though the observable event is identical. Because the intention is different in each case, they are different actions. Taylor's argument is that since the agent's intentions were different in each situation, the situations are different. If these situations are different, and intentions are causes (as Davidson claims), then we should be able to account for the difference solely in terms of cause and effect. The situations are different because there is a different intention in each one, but we cannot account for the difference in terms of cause and effect. Different intentions produced identical events. The differences between the situations can only be explained in terms of intentions. Therefore, intentions are not causes.

In light of the arguments of Margolis and Taylor against Davidson, it is clear that what the action is cannot be reduced to what is observed. In addition to the overt observable act, an accurate description must include the intention, that is, the belief that explains the act.

Intention

The intention is the primary element in an action, at least as far as a moral evaluation is concerned. This means that a consideration of the intention alone could determine the moral worth of the action. Since the intention is primary, it must be considered before you take into account the motive and circumstances.

Actions fall into three moral categories: obligatory, permissible, or impermissible. To determine whether the action is morally obligatory, permissible, or impermissible, the intention must be measured against the principle of respect for persons. If the intention conforms to the principle, it is a good intention.

For example, suppose a medical doctor has purchased a life insurance policy on a certain patient. Knowing that this patient is allergic to a certain medication, the physician decides to prescribe this medication. The plan is that the medication will kill the patient so that the doctor can collect the insurance money in order to start an orphanage. Applied professional ethics suggests that we begin the moral analysis with the intention and then proceed to consider the motive and the circumstances. Since the intention of killing violates the principle of respect, the act is morally impermissible. This one criterion exhausts the moral analysis with regard to determining the moral permissibility of the act. Wrong is wrong. A good motive or peculiar circumstances cannot make a morally wrong action right.

Now consider this example. Suppose you are deciding whether you should move out of your apartment and buy a house. The first step in morally analyzing the act is to determine the intention. Your intention is to purchase a house. The second step is to determine whether the intention is morally obligatory, permissible or impermissible. The principle of respect does not morally oblige you to buy a house, but neither does it forbid it. The intention is permissible, assuming that the purchase is fair and just.

If the intention is impermissible, then your moral analysis of the action can stop. You must not act on this intention. Or, if the intention is obligatory, then you must act on it. But many intentions are morally permissible. The principle of respect neither requires nor forbids them. In this case, if the intention is permissible, you must continue your moral analysis so as to include the motive and circumstances.

Motive

The motive is the long term goal of the act. The same intention can be done for various motives. For example, suppose you flick the lights on and off. To understand what the act is, we must focus on the intention. The belief that explains this particular act is that turning the lights on and off in this way will get someone's attention. It could be a method of testing the lights, but this is an act of getting someone's attention.

Again, the motive is the long term goal of the act. In this case, your motive might be to notify a security guard that you need help. Or, it could be to notify your partner in a bank robbery that the security guard is sleeping. Both of these acts have the same intention, getting someone's attention. The difference between them is a difference in motive, not intention.

In these examples, the intention is permissible. Getting someone's attention with a flashing light is morally allowed. Therefore, the moral analysis has to move beyond the intention to consider the motive. The motive in the first case, to notify a security guard that you need help, is good, since it flows from the principle of respect. But the motive in the second case, to notify your partner in a bank robbery that the security guard is sleeping, is not. Getting someone's attention for the sake of carrying out an injustice is morally wrong.

Suppose that a physician intends to diagnose a patient's disease by sending a sample to a clinical lab. This is a good intention. If the motive is to serve the best interest of the patient, then there is both a good intention and a good motive. But if it turns out that the physician owns stock in the lab, it is possible that the doctor's sole motive in diagnosing the disease is to increase the lab's profits. In this case, the motive may so affect the action that the good intention becomes morally worthless.

We are not implying that profits are impermissible. But as we have seen in Chapter Two, when there is a conflict between one's self-interest and one's role as a professional, one's professional role carries more moral weight than one's self-interest.

Suppose this physician intends to diagnose a disease by sending a sample to a clinical lab, and the motive is to promote the welfare of the patient, but it happens that the lab is known to be chronically incompetent. The prudent professional will see that even though there is a good intention and a good motive, the circumstances may not warrant the action.

Circumstances

The circumstances are the concrete, peculiar conditions within which you carry out your action. Although the circumstances do not by themselves determine the moral worth of an action, they do play a significant role in applying moral principles to concrete situations.

Our ethical lives are not lived out in the abstract. Morality is more than theory, since every action is done in a particular situation with its own unique conditions. Some people overemphasize this fact. Indeed, one entire theory of ethics states that actions are good or bad based solely on a consideration of the situation in which the action is performed.[6] One problem with overemphasizing the situation is that it becomes impossible to determine what is morally relevant within the situation. It is fine to say that you should look at the individual characteristics of the situation, but what are you looking for? Without any moral principles, there is no clear guideline to help you focus on morally relevant factors.

On the other hand, it is possible to place too little emphasis on the circumstances. A prudent application of principles takes into account the circumstances unique to each case. For example, in general, the principle of justice requires that you should return what you have borrowed. But suppose you have borrowed your neighbor's shotgun and he comes to your house in a rage demanding his gun back so that he can shoot his wife. In these circumstances, prudence would suggest that it would not be just to return it under these conditions. In this way, the circumstances can change an otherwise good act into an unwarranted one.

Notice that the circumstances did not warrant breaking the principle of justice. Rather, a prudent consideration of the circumstances surrounding the case helped to define what the just act is.

Intermediate Summary

There are three important factors in applying moral principles to actual cases. First, the intention must be good. Second, the motive must be good. Third, the circumstances must warrant the action.

A good motive cannot make a bad intention good. However, a bad motive can detract from the moral worth of a good intention.

Likewise, unusual circumstances do not justify a bad intention or a bad motive. However, a good intention with a good motive may be unwarranted in certain circumstances. This is where prudence plays its role, in helping to determine how to apply good intentions and good motives to particular circumstances. See Diagram 3 on p. 72.

Moral Principles and Empirical Facts

Moral knowledge includes more than a familiarity with abstract principles. It involves a knowledge of particular facts. This consideration is especially important in professional ethics. Professionalism requires competence. This means knowing the skills relevant to your professional area, but also knowing the contingencies surrounding each case. Medical doctors often need to know when the patient last ate. Engineers, such as those working on the space shuttle, often need to know the weather conditions surrounding the construction and operation of the object being designed. These pieces of information are empirical facts that are relevant to a moral decision.

Practical moral decision-making often involves a reasoning process that combines moral principles with empirical facts. The conclusion of this reasoning process is a decision that calls for an action.

Diagram 3

Applying Moral Principles

Intention

1. Determine the intention. The intention is the belief that explains the action.

2. Measure the intention against the moral principles that flow from the principle of respect.

3. Determine if the intention is obligatory, permissible, or impermissible.

4. If the intention is permissible, go on to analyze the motive and circumstances.

Motive

1. Determine the motive. The motive is the long term goal of the action.

2. Measure the motive against the moral principles that flow from the principle of respect.

3. Determine if the motive is obligatory, permissible, or impermissible.

4. If the motive is permissible, go on to analyze the circumstances.

Circumstances

1. Examine the circumstances.

2. Ascertain the relevant empirical facts.

3. Using prudence, determine whether the circumstances warrant the action.

Middle Level Principles

Moral principles are sometimes so abstract that it is not easy to see how they apply to particular cases. One might ask "How is respect for persons expressed in this particular case?"

In applying principles to the facts and circumstances of a particular case, it is helpful to think in terms of middle level moral principles. These are moral guidelines that are at an intermediate level of abstraction. They are not so removed from the concrete particulars that it is difficult to see how they apply. On the other hand, they are abstract enough that they apply to a relatively broad range of factual circumstances.

For example, a profession's code of ethics will specify how the general principle of respect is applied to that profession. The National Society of Professional Engineers' Code of Ethics lists five fundamental canons stating that engineers shall:

1. Hold paramount the safety, health and welfare of the public in the performance of their professional duties.

2. Perform services only in areas of their competence.

3. Issue public statements only in an objective and truthful manner.

4. Act in professional matters for each employer or client as faithful agents or trustees.

5. Avoid improper solicitation of professional employment.

Similarly, the International Council of Nurses' International Code of Nursing Ethics, the AMA's Principles of Medical Ethics and other professional codes represent middle level principles. Such codes of ethics do not exhaust all of the middle level principles. Instead, their role is to provide guidelines that flow from the fundamental principle of respect, and to address the most common situations and relationships faced in one's profession. It remains for the individual to use prudence in applying these general guidelines to each specific case.

Prudence

Prudence is practical wisdom. It is the ability to apply moral principles to specific cases. People are not born with this ability. It is developed through experience in making moral decisions.

Just as athletic ability can be improved through physical training, and musical skill can be augmented through repetition, prudence is a habit that can be developed with practice. Good decisions pave the way for more good decisions.

Conclusion

As you study cases, it may at first be difficult to discern the appropriate application of moral principles. But with practice, you can develop prudence so that it will become easier to recognize the relevant aspects needed for a clear moral analysis, including the intention, motive and circumstances.

Diagram 4

Moral Decision-Making

General Moral Principles

These are the abstract moral principles that guide moral decision making at Level Three.

These include the principles of:

Respect
Non-malevolence
Benevolence
Integrity
Justice
Utility
Double Effect

Middle Level Principles

These are moral guidelines that are at an intermediate level of abstraction. More concrete than the general moral principles, they are abstract enough to apply to a relatively broad range of factual circumstances.

Professional Codes of Ethics often contain examples of middle level principles.

Moral Decisions

The moral decision looks for guidance from general moral principles and middle level principles. and then prudently determines how these apply to the concrete particulars of the case at hand.

Questions for Review and Discussion

1. What is the problem of applying principles to concrete cases? How do intermediate principles help in this process?

2. Why is it important to properly describe the act?

3. What is the difference between intention and motive as described in the chapter?

4. Why is it important to maintain the order: intention, motive, circumstance?

5. Can circumstances make an otherwise good action bad or an otherwise bad action good?

6. Describe the role of prudence in moral decision-making.

Notes to Chapter Five

1. Carol Gilligan, *In Another Voice*.

2. Donald Davidson, "Actions, Reasons and Causes," *The Journal of Philosophy* 60 (1963).

3. *Ibid*., p. 686.

4. Joseph Margolis, "Explanation by Reasons and by Causes," *The Journal of Philosophy* LXVII 7 (1970) 188.

5. Richard Taylor, *Action and Purpose*. (Prentice Hall: Englewood Cliffs, NJ, 1966), p. 253.

6. Joseph Fletcher, *Situation Ethics: The New Morality*. (Philadelphia: Westminster Press, 1966).

Chapter 6

Conflicts in Rules and Relationships

Suppose you are a manager in a company that is considering moving a factory to a foreign country. There are strong economic incentives for the move. Foreign labor is inexpensive and regulatory laws are less strict in the prospective country. The expected result of the move is that labor costs could be reduced and management streamlined thus increasing profits and the value of the company's stock. As part of your retirement package, you own stock in the corporation.

It can also be expected that there will be several negative impacts from the move. The local economy depends heavily on the factory. The workers and their families, along with those of the service sector near the factory, will lose their income if the factory moves.

Here is your conflict. You are faced with an obligation to the shareholders of the corporation that employs you, and since you are also a shareholder, it is in your interest to promote the company's welfare. You have a stake in the company. Further, the company expects you to make decisions that will maximize profits. You also have an obligation to your family. They expect you to continue to help provide for them. Additionally, you have an obligation to the community. They expect you to be loyal.

The conflict in this case is between the interests, roles, and principles that make up the moral situation in all of its complexity. Your interests as an employee may conflict with your interests as a shareholder. Your role as a parent and spouse may conflict with your role as an effective manager. Your interests as a shareholder may conflict with your role as a citizen.

This is a modern example of a dilemma that has its roots in ancient Greek moral reflections as expressed in classical drama and literature.

In Sophocles' *Antigone*, she has to figure out how to balance her role as a family member with her role as a citizen. In Plato's *Euthyphro*, Euthyphro is faced with a conflict between his interests in advancing his career, his role as a citizen, and his loyalty to his family based on his role as a son. There are similar conflicts in a number of Shakespeare's plays, including *Hamlet*, *Romeo and Juliet*, *The Tempest*, and others.

Conflict Resolution and Moral Development

The wisdom of these stories is that they give concrete examples of conflicts and attempts at conflict resolution. The moral life is always made up of conflicts. It is a common mistake to think that conflicts are to be avoided.

The ways in which you confront conflicts will shape your personal development. This is an important aspect of Kohlberg's theory of moral development. The child who is never challenged to think of others, who never faces the conflict between self-interest and the interest of the group, will never grow and develop morally. The adolescent that is never challenged to look beyond his or her own group may never grow to develop respect for all human beings. Without conflict, there is no growth. So in this way, conflict plays are crucial role in moral growth and development.

In Chapter Two, we discussed several cases that involved conflicts between interests, roles and principles. In your case studies, you will see how others have been confronted with conflict.[1] And in your own professional career, you will be faced with complex situations filled with conflicting demands.

Conflict is not the only way that moral growth and development can occur. When you hear stories of moral heroes, or meet individuals that set a clear moral example, you can model your behavior after theirs. But even then, you will be learning from the way these moral heroes faced conflict wisely.

The conflicts that you will face, both in your case studies and in your actual cases, will provide opportunities for moral growth and the development of professional responsibility. By prudently confronting conflicts, a person becomes a responsible professional.

Dialogue

Recent developments in ethical theory have focused on the importance of dialogue in clarifying principles and making sense of cases.[2] Of course, dialogue is not completely new in the moral life. Socrates spent his life in dialogue with his contemporaries asking questions about how to live well. What is new is the emphasis on dialogue.

Moral development takes place within the context of a dialogue that includes several tensions made possible by an underlying commonality. There is a tension between the individual and the family, the family and the society, traditional moral perspectives and new needs or possibilities. The dialogue is carried out in an atmosphere with a specific kind of tension.

In order for dialogue to be possible, there must be the tension that comes from differing perspectives. But it is also necessary to have a common ground. In order to talk, people must share a language. For dialogue to occur, there must be some shared experience and vocabulary. In the contemporary world, this involves an openness to the common heritage of moral discourse found in the tradition of world literature, its dramas, stories and examples of moral reasoning.

> To risk conversation with our classic texts should be more like meeting such characters as Amos and Isaiah, Ruth and Jeremiah, Oedipus and Antigone, even Medea and Herakles. . . They expose our present inauthenticity and complacency. At the same time, they also force us to resist their own half-concealed tragic flaws.[3]

Moral discourse involves discussion with our contemporaries as well as with our traditions. It is healthy to promote this kind of tension and "tense-ness" in a vital moral discourse. As such, this dialogue is open to a plurality of views.

The very practice of dialogue fosters respect for persons, because it requires that you listen. Listening to those around you, as well as to your cultural heritage, is part of your responsibility. To be a responsible professional is to respond to the world in which you live and work in all of its dimensions. This involves listening, and then taking part in the dialogue. It involves being attentive to more than the narrow technical aspects of your profession: mathematical formulas, physiological processes, mechanical structures, and market forces. The attentive, responsive professional listens to individual concerns, responds to community needs, and attends to the human and social impact of each decision.

There are two extreme responses besides dialogue: fight or flight. The fight response is essentially an assertion of one's interests in the face of conflicting moral claims. This is an offensive response. You go on the attack and become a bully. Conversely, the flight response is conflict avoidance. If your attention is focused on one narrow aspect of a problem, you may end up avoiding the human and moral issues involved. For example, there is a common temptation to ignore the human element by reducing a problem to its technical features. As a result, your decision may be technically feasible, though since you have avoided the real moral issue, the conflict may grow worse, exacerbated by technical misadventures.

The appropriate response for a professional is to avoid these extremes and to face the dilemma squarely. To enter into dialogue is to recognize that there are always conflicting claims that need to be adjudicated in any moral decision. There are personal interests, social roles and moral principles that must be balanced. Dialogue is the appropriate response of a professional to moral conflict, and is central to the post-conventional level of moral decision-making.

Conflict Resolution and "Unresolved" Cases

There is a natural, human desire for clarity and precision in solving problems. Some kinds of problems do, in fact, lend themselves to mathematical precision. As a professional, you will face certain technical problems that lend themselves to exact solutions. On the other hand, you will face many problems that, though they do not have one single, precise solution, have a range of possible acceptable solutions. Each of these may have certain advantages and disadvantages, though the professional community will recognize these alternatives as acceptable and within the limits of professional behavior. Often times, there are non-technical criteria that must be taken into account in choosing among those possibilities.

Moral reasoning does not exhibit the same degree of precision as mathematical reasoning.[4] Because of this, some cases will not yield a clean, precise solution. Often times, moral dilemmas involve tragic consequences, so that no matter what one decides, the outcome of the case ends up being less than fully desirable. This is part of human living. Life is sometimes tragic.

In the Heinz dilemma, we proposed a resolution in Chapter Two based upon the principle of respect for persons. In our resolution, we stated that Heinz should take the drug, but that he should be willing to face the social sanctions for stealing. This entails that he might have to go to jail, an outcome that would be tragic.

This is what makes the dilemma a dilemma. A moral dilemma does not mean that there is no right action. Instead, the right action (or actions) may entail undesirable consequences.

For example, a real life dilemma in medical ethics involves the problem of treating a pregnant woman who has cancer of the uterus. The normal treatment for cancer of the uterus is to perform a hysterectomy. This would remove the cancer from the woman's body. When the woman is pregnant, the operation would also entail removing the fetus. As the principle of double effect would suggest, carrying out the operation is the right thing to do. Still, it has tragic consequences. This case has a morally permissible solution, but it has a foreseeable tragic outcome.

Morality is not mathematics. This case is *not* solved by doing a cost-benefit analysis of weighing one life against another. The case of the woman with cancer of the uterus should be approached with the principle of respect. This involves something different from mathematical values, namely the dignity and worth of the individual as a human being. The intention of the treatment is to treat the pregnant woman with respect and cure her of the cancer. The foreseeable side effect is measured against the good intended effect. The final moral decision, then, is based on qualitative factors determined by prudence, and is not simply reducible to a quantitative calculus.

Rules and Relationships

The significance of dialogue, as we have described it, contributes to the debate between Kohlberg and Gilligan, as well as to the broader social debate raised by certain feminists between rule-based ethics and an ethics of care that focuses on relationships. Dialogue promotes a more holistic, balanced approach to moral decision-making, which includes both procedural considerations having to do with justice, and matters of content having to do with the good life.

We have already seen in Chapter Two that the moral life includes conflicts. We focused on conflicts in self-interest, social roles and moral principles. There can be conflicting interests, or conflicts between interests and roles. Likewise, there can be conflicting roles, or conflicts between roles and moral principles. We showed how Kohlberg's theory of moral development can be used to give order to these conflicts.

In Chapter Three, we showed how the traditional, masculine way of formulating moral guidelines can turn ethics into a mere matter of rule-following. Carol Gilligan's criticism of Kohlberg focused on this tendency.

The "masculine" ethic that overemphasizes rules is flawed because it does not provide a principled way of resolving conflicts between rules. To resolve conflicts between rules, what is needed is a dialogue that moves beyond rules to discuss the human, social context in order to provide content to the rules. An ethic that focuses on rules becomes a "rule-maintaining" or even "rule-worshipping" ethic. Respect for the individual person is forgotten as the rule becomes more important than the individual and human social relationships.[5]

Likewise, the "feminine" ethic that overemphasizes relationships is flawed because it does not provide a principled way of resolving conflicts between relationships. Furthermore, an ethic that focuses on relationships can become a "relationship-maintaining" ethic. This can be unhealthy, insofar as some relationships can be debilitating or even addictive. Maintaining such relationships does not foster human dignity. To resolve a conflict between two relationships, or to assess a specific relationship, it is necessary to promote a dialogue that includes a discussion of the principle of respect. Through this sort of dialogue, one can move beyond a relationship-maintaining posture to an ethic that *promotes* healthy human relationships.

Finally, the dialogue that we are encouraging is a discourse that is open to the concerns expressed in a rule-based (typically masculine) ethic and those expressed in a relationship-based (typically feminine) ethic. A fuller understanding of the moral life and the place of the principle of respect in applied professional ethics can be achieved as a result of the interaction of these two perspectives.

Friendship and Justice

The moral tradition in the West has taken account of both friendship and justice. Aristotle described the relationship between justice and friendship in his reflections on the good life.

> Friendship would seem to hold cities together . . . If people are friends, they have no need of justice, but if they are just they need friendship in addition; and the justice that is most just seems to belong to friendship.[6]

This illustrates a complementary relationship between friendship and justice, between relationships and rules.

Professional life involves rules, but it also takes place within a social context. That social context is only possible when individuals exhibit a concern for the well-being of others. Kohlberg's theory of moral development suggests that moral maturity involves moving beyond the narcissistic concern for oneself to a broader concern for one's community, and ultimately for all persons.

Of course, it is not possible to have an intimate friendship with every single human being on earth. However, it is possible as a professional to act with concern for the well-being of other individuals and the public at large.

For example, a medical professional can and should be concerned with the welfare of his or her patients, and indeed, public health in general. An engineer must be concerned with the impact of a product's design on those who produce it, use it and all those affected by it. In professional ethics, this concern for the well-being of others should be understood as an extension of the kind of concern that one feels for friends.

Conclusion

What should you do if you are a manager of a factory that is considering moving to a foreign country, as in the case we described at the beginning of this chapter?

The first step in analyzing the case is to identify the various conflicts that make up the problem. What are the interests, social roles, and moral principles involved in the case? Is there a genuine conflict in rules, in relationships, or between rules and relationships?

The second step is to face the conflict through dialogue. Here it is important to judiciously order the interests, roles, and principles governing the decision. Kohlberg's theory shows that interests are morally meaningful when they are subordinated to social roles. Likewise, social roles are morally meaningful when they are subordinated to the principle of respect.

Finally, the process of dialogue implies that there may be more than one solution to some cases and sometimes even the best solution will entail tragic consequences. Of course, we should always work to reduce tragic outcomes, though in some cases an element of tragedy may be unavoidable.

Dialogue also implies that moral decisions develop in an ongoing process of reflection and revision. The study of applied professional ethics should encourage you to face moral conflicts in a manner that promotes healthy dialogue.

Questions for Review and Discussion

1. When is conflict good or healthy?

2. When is conflict bad?

3. How does dialogue contribute to resolving the tension between a masculine ethic of rules and a feminine ethic of relationships?

4. What would you do if you were in the situation described at the beginning of this chapter? What are the relevant factors that might alter your decision?

Notes to Chapter Six

1. See Albert R. Jonsen and Stephen Toulmin, *The Abuse of Casuistry: A History of Moral Reasoning*. (Berkeley and Los Angeles: University of California Press, 1988).

2. For example, see Robert Bellah, et. al, *Habits of the Heart* and *The Good Society*.

3. David Tracy, *Plurality and Ambiguity*. (New York: Harper and Row, 1987), pp. 86-7. Quoted in Robert Bellah, et. al., The Good Society. (New York: Alfred A. Knopf, 1991), p. 323, n. 42.

4. Aristotle, *Nichomachean Ethics*, Book I, Chap. 2.

5. Kierkegaard makes a similar point, claiming that an ethic that places too much emphasis on universal rules subordinates the concrete individual to an abstraction. See Kierkegaard, *Fear and Trembling*.

6. Aristotle, *Nichomachean Ethics*, 1155a23-28.

Chapter 7

Context and Character

Applied professional ethics is a complicated but orderly mixture of theory and practice. Anyone who has acquired professional skills knows that theory without practice is useless.

Theory and Practice

There is a famous old saying, "It works in theory, but it doesn't work in practice." This criticism of useless, abstract theorizing expresses an attitude shared by both professional ethics and professional practice. You can't divorce theory from practice.

This is the main point of one of the classics of German philosophy, Immanuel Kant's *Critique of Pure Reason*. Abstract theory without content is empty. At the same time, data without structure is blind. True knowledge always contains a mixture of reason and experience, of theory and practice.[1]

Our book represents the theoretical aspect of applied professional ethics. It provides the orderly structure within which actual cases can be analyzed. But without looking at actual cases, someone who studied only this book would have theory without practice. This kind of pure knowledge is not typical of professionals.

The very nature of professional knowledge provides an opportunity for bringing together theoretical knowledge and practical applications. Physicians study anatomy to better diagnose and treat patients. Engineers study mathematics and physics to produce better designs. So the theoretical framework set forth in this book should be complemented with the study of cases.

Cases and Contexts

Case studies are useful in professional education to develop this applied knowledge. They are used in business schools, law schools, medical schools, engineering programs, and in virtually every area of professional education. Cases provide a concrete context to see how a theory works in practice.

It is mistaken to think that one area of professional ethics is fundamentally different from another. For example, there is not a completely separate set of ethical standards for business and for medicine. Of course, the conventions and social expectations of each profession may vary slightly, but this is a Level Two difference, not a Level Three difference. The basic framework of moral development and respect for persons applies in every area of professional ethics. An understanding of Kohlberg's levels of moral development shows that the difference between various areas of professional ethics is not a fundamental difference in principles, but a difference in application. Medical ethics applies moral principles to medicine, while business ethics applies the very same moral principles to business. The basic framework set forth in this text can be applied to cases in various areas of professional ethics.

This book should be used in conjunction with case studies in your area of expertise. Appendix 5 contains case study books in professional ethics. Appendix 3 gives ideas about ways to write your own case studies, and appendix 4 gives samples of student case study reports. With practice, you will get better at applying professional ethics to the context of actual cases, so that you will develop the habit of making wise, practical decisions.

As you look at each case, it will help to make yourself aware of the social context of the case. What is its history? Are there cultural factors that are of significant influence? Are there subtle specifics of this case that make it essentially different from other apparently similar cases? These are some of the circumstances that should be taken into account along with an evaluation of the intention and motive guiding one's action.[2]

Kohlberg's theory suggests that social context is not by itself an adequate basis for mature moral decision-making. However, those at Level Two, those who base their moral judgments on social expectations and obligations, will be tempted to say that context makes all the difference. So, for applied professional ethics, while you can not understand the case without its social context, you can not make a moral judgment without a guiding principle. In that way, the social context is subordinated to the unvarying principles of applied professional ethics.

Hence, while Level Two is inadequate in itself as a perspective for moral decision-making, it is valuable in that it urges us to look at the moral influence of social institutions. An awareness of the social context is important since it might happen that moral conflicts may arise out of institutionalized structures. Some social structures promote good, moral behavior, while others may encourage moral corruption.

For example, the strict line-of-command management model is notorious for contributing to moral failure. In this context, when subordinates suspect their immediate superior of wrong-doing, they have no one to report the problem to except that superior. This situation tends to lead employees into collusion with their superiors. It is not only individual behavior that needs to be changed, but the command structure itself.[3]

Level Three incorporates the insights gained about the influence of social structure on moral development, but it also provides a critical test to evaluate the health of a social context. The principle of respect is a stable moral guide. It does not change, but with prudence one must look at the varied contexts to decide what respect means in each case, and how to achieve excellence in each context. As Aristotle put it,

> It is hard work to be excellent, since in each case it is hard work to find what is intermediate . . . Getting angry, or giving and spending money, is easy and anyone can do it; but doing it to the right person, in the right amount, at the right time, for the right end, and in the right way is no longer easy, nor can everyone do it.[4]

Often times it is difficult to know what is the right thing to do. This is because the case may look different depending on the perspective of the one looking at the case and the moral level from which it is viewed.

For example, consider the Meris Laboratories case referred to in Chapter Two. We looked at that case from two perspectives. From the Level One perspective of self-interest, it appeared to be a conflict of interest case. There is no genuine resolution to the case from this perspective. From the Level Two perspective of social roles, the problem appeared in a new light. In this way, a different perspective can change the appearance of the case in which a decision must be made.

Our emphasis on contexts stems from the root meaning of the word "context." The word literally means "to weave together." This includes coherently integrating the environment or setting of a case. We have argued that Kohlberg's approach helps us to balance the many concerns involved in a moral decision. The context includes the interests, roles, and principles of the case as well as the specific historical setting, the social and cultural environment, and a living dialogue with the tradition of moral discourse.

Balancing Perspectives

This reflection on the context of decision-making leads to the insight that a balanced moral life is desirable. The moral life flows smoothly when it is in one's self-interest to maintain social expectations and when those social expectations are for you to treat others with respect. One company that seems to have accomplished this is Southwestern Airlines. At Southwestern, there seems to be a fairly successful balance between self-interest, social conformity and respect for persons. Through a profit sharing program, it is in an employee's self-interest to work hard to promote the well-being of the company. And there is a strong sense of community within the organization that presumes that the group can be maintained and strengthened by providing safe, inexpensive transportation for its customers. In this climate, it is in the interest of the employee who finds a safety problem to report it. It is socially expected, and it is one's moral duty.

The moral life begins to break down and can be frustrated when social institutions exist that bring an individual's interests, roles and principles into conflict. For example, Richard Feynam, a physicist who worked on the Rogers Commission that investigated the Space Shuttle disaster, found that NASA's problem went deeper than a faulty O-ring.[5] He found that the American space program had developed a sort of corporate culture where individuals were reluctant to report problems. The social pressure for success in the Space Shuttle program had become so great that employees found it punitive to report safety problems. Instead of an environment that welcomed safety concerns, the social mood denigrated any criticism, even if it was constructive. So the moral duty to report safety problems was in conflict with the employee's self-interest. The social climate failed to balance self-interest with moral principle so that the two would be mutually supporting.

The challenge of balancing perspectives is to align self-interest and social conformity with moral principles. When moral obligation conflicts with self-interest, there is a test of character to see if you can subordinate your own interests to the respect due others. However, there is a limit to the psychological strain of having to continually act in a selfless way. If these perspectives are balanced, then the demands of moral duty should contribute to self-actualization.

This alignment of interest, roles and principles does not reduce ethics to selfishness. There is no invisible moral hand. The pursuit of selfish desires is not automatically identical with moral duty. Nonetheless, it is desirable for professionals to situate themselves in circumstances where respecting persons is personally fulfilling and socially valued. The balanced moral life weaves together self-interest, social conformity and moral principles.

Moral Character

The "weaving together" theme applies not only to context, but also to questions of moral character. Here, the notion of integrity mirrors the concern for balance just described. To have integrity means to hold together in a coherent manner all of the particular actions making up a whole life.

How is character formed? Aristotle recognized that moral character is formed through habit. Even contemporary psychologists, with their theories of personality development, support this idea. Just as good eating habits and exercise lead to health, while poor eating habits and inactivity lead to ill-health, the exercise of good decision-making leads to the development of sound moral character. This is similar to the development of good mental habits that are required for problem-solving. Habit shapes character. The improvement of character comes from repeatedly making good decisions. A well formed character, or a person with virtue, is shaped by habitually performing good actions that avoid extremes and aim at moderation. A simple example of how character is formed by habit can be seen in the heroic fire fighter. Fire fighters often report that what appears to us as great courage appears to them as a spontaneous action. This is so because their training is so thorough that this kind of action becomes second nature to them. Through training, they habitually learn to avoid being either foolhardy or cowardly. Good training involves repetition that aims at moderation while avoiding excess, imprudently doing too much, and deficiency, passively doing too little. And with repetition their character is formed so that it becomes easier and easier to be successful in their tasks.[6]

The art of living well involves habitually making good choices. But how do you know what a good choice is? A good choice is one that conforms to the principle of respect for persons, that is, one in which you treat yourself and others with the respect and dignity befitting a person. You know that a choice is a good one if it is consistent with your other choices, since this is a good test of integrity. A good choice is one that brings coherence to your life.

A typical image of a life lacking in coherence is what we commonly think of as a person who leads a "double life." Such a person is concerned with giving the outward appearance of acceptable behavior, though when no one is looking, this person acts otherwise. There are other kinds of moral hypocrisy. Even those who completely devote themselves to what is apparently one thing, like money or pleasure, in fact end up living a double life. For, as Kierkegaard has pointed out, as soon as they get the one thing they think they want, they look for something else.[7] The lack of coherence in the person who leads this kind of double life stems from the fact that there is no universal principle that might serve as a source of coherence.

To make moral decisions from the Level Three perspective requires a commitment, a choice. You can grow through Level One to Level Two, passing through the first four and a half stages that Kohlberg describes. This is a natural, psychological development. The first two levels do not require a deliberate decision. However, entrance into the Level Three perspective of moral decision-making only comes when there is a conscious choice to adopt a universal moral principle. For this reason, Level Three is most appropriate to professional life. Professional life itself requires that one make a conscious commitment to a standard of excellence.

The Level Three perspective entails accepting one's life-task. This means taking responsibility for yourself and your life. What does it mean to take responsibility? The most fundamental meaning of responsibility is to respond to others. So to take responsibility for yourself and your life means to respond appropriately to your life situations and to others. This is why the highest principle of Level Three is respect for persons. The principle of respect serves as a guide to determine what choices and actions are appropriate for responsible persons.

The way to understand the meaning of a life-task is to appreciate the concept of a "fundamental option" or "dominant concern." The commitment to excellence and the principle of respect for persons should be the dominant concern of the life of a professional. Professionalism entails a unified focus on excellence. This entails both high technical standards and high moral standards. To be successful in professional life includes living out one's dominant concern for maintaining high standards.

Actions are not simply discrete units that can be understood in isolation. Rather, each act is a part that forms the larger pattern of your life and reveals the fundamental option guiding it. Everyday acts of honesty reinforce the dominant concern for excellence in professional life. However, taking home a few office supplies, for example, or illicitly accepting "gifts," can form a pattern that detracts from the dominant concern for human dignity.

Just as great acts of virtue flow from individuals who have established good habits, gross acts of corruption usually flow from a pattern of petty indiscretions.

Making a habit of being honest, courageous and benevolent, and acting with integrity, builds one's character so that it becomes easier and even enjoyable to do good actions. As healthy physical exercise is enjoyable to one who is in good physical condition, sound moral actions are enjoyable to one who is in good moral shape. Developing good habits - that is, virtue - comes by forming one's character so that one can function effectively as a professional. And while enjoyment is not the goal of virtue, the enjoyment and fulfillment of the moral life is one of the beneficial effects of living well.

Conclusion

Applied professional ethics employs moral theory in the service of bringing moral order to professional life. The cases you will study are a representation of professional life. They will help you to reflect on the moral element of your professional obligations. But ethics is more than an abstract exercise in thought. It deals with concrete cases, and with practice, will have the effect of shaping your character. These cases, and the way you respond to them, should also help shape your response to real life problems. The nexus of theory and practice in the moral sphere is habit. To be a professional means to develop good moral habits. This includes the habit of treating people with respect and using your professional skills with care.

Questions for Review and Discussion

1. Describe how the relationship between theory and practice is reflected in professional activity.

2. Explain how the relationship between theory and practice is reflected in the relationship between a moral framework and actual cases.

3. What is included in the context (environment or setting) of a moral decision?

4. Give examples of social institutions that have successfully balanced interests, roles and principles. Name some that you do not think have accomplished this balance.

5. How is the development of moral character related to the principle of integrity?

6. What is the dominant concern in your life? What should it be?

7. Explain how Kohlberg's theory provides a common moral vocabulary helpful for moral decision-making in applied professional ethics.

Notes to Chapter Seven

1. Immanuel Kant, *The Critique of Pure Reason.* Trans. by Norman Kemp Smith. (New York: St. Martin's Press, 1965). Kant also wrote a small piece titled *On the Old Saw: That May be Right in Theory but it Won't Work in Practice.* Trans. E.B. Ashton. (Philadelphia, University of Pennsylvania Press, 1974).

2. The role of circumstances was discussed in Chapter Five.

3. For examples of how social structures can affect individual moral behavior, see James Waters, "Catch 20.5: Corporate Morality as an Organizational Phenomenon," in *Contemporary Moral Controversies in Business*, Ed. A. Pablo Iannone, (Oxford: Oxford University Press, 1989), pp. 151-163. Besides strict line of command, Waters lists other common organization blocks: strong role models, task group cohesiveness, ambiguity about priorities, separation of decisions, division of work, protection from outside intervention.

4. Aristotle, *Nichomachean Ethics*, 1109a24-29.

5. Richard Feynman, *What do You Care What Other People Think? Further Adventures of a Curious Character*, as told to Ralph Leighton, New York: W.W. Norton and Co., 1988.

6. Aristotle, *Nichamachean Ethics*. Book II, Chapter 6. Notice that what is moderate for one individual may be excessive for another. The rational mean varies from individual to individual based on, among other things, their degree of training and experience.

7. This is the theme of Kierkegaard's *Either/Or*, vol. 1, though he makes the point more explicitly in *Purity of Heart is to Will One Thing*.

Appendix 1

Codes of Professional Ethics

This appendix contains the following ten codes of professional ethics:

1. The Hippocratic Oath
2. American Medical Association's Principles of Medical Ethics
3. American Nurses Association Code for Nurses
4. American Psychological Association's Ethical Principles of Psychologists
5. The Nuremberg Code
6. Code of Ethics of Engineers (Accreditation Board for Engineering and Technology)
7. Code of Ethics for Engineers (National Society of Professional Engineers)
8. American Bar Association's Model Rules of Professional Conduct (Preamble: A Lawyer's Responsibilities)
9. Standards of Ethical Conduct for Management Accountants
10. Code of Ethics of Financial Executives Institute

1. Hippocratic Oath[1]

I swear by Apollo Physician and Asclepius and Hygieia and Panacea and all the gods and goddesses, making them my witness, that I will fulfil according to my ability and judgment this oath and this covenant:

To hold him who has taught me this art as equal to my parents and to live my life in partnership with him, and if he is in need of money to give him a share of mine, and to regard his offspring as equal to my brothers in male lineage and to teach them this art--if they desire to learn it--without fee and covenant; to give a share of precepts and oral instruction and all the other learning to my sons and to the sons of him who has instructed me and to pupils who have signed the covenant and have taken an oath according to the medical law, but to no one else.

I will apply dietetic measures for the benefit of the sick according to my ability and judgment; I will keep them from harm and injustice.

I will neither give a deadly drug to anybody if asked for it, nor will I make a suggestion to this effect. Similarly I will not give to a woman an abortive remedy. In purity and holiness I will guard my life and my art.

I will not use the knife, not even on sufferers from stone, but will withdraw in favor of such men as are engaged in this work.

Whatever houses I may visit, I will come for the benefit of the sick, remaining free of all intentional injustice, of all mischief and in particular of sexual relations with both female and male persons, be they free or slaves.

What I may see or hear in the course of the treatment or even outside of the treatment in regard to the life of men, which on no account one must spread abroad, I will keep to myself holding such things shameful to be spoken about.

If I fulfill this oath and do not violate it, may it be granted to me to enjoy life and art, being honored with fame among all men for all time to come; if I transgress it and swear falsely, may the opposite of all this be my lot.

2. American Medical Association's Principles of Medical Ethics[2]

Preamble

The medical profession has long subscribed to a body of ethical statements developed primarily for the benefit of the patient. As a member of this profession, a physician must recognize responsibility not only to patients, but also to society, to other health professionals, and to self. The following Principles adopted by the American Medical Association are not laws, but standards of conduct which define the essentials of honorable behavior for the physician.

I. A physician shall be dedicated to providing competent medical service with compassion and respect for human dignity.

II. A physician shall deal honestly with patients and colleagues, and strive to expose those physicians deficient in character or competence, or who engage in fraud or deception.

III. A physician shall respect the law and also recognize a responsibility to seek changes in those requirements which are contrary to the best interests of the patient.

IV, A physician shall respect the rights of patients, of colleagues, and of other health professionals, and shall safeguard patient confidences within the constraints of the law.

V. A physician shall continue to study, apply and advance scientific knowledge, make relevant information available to patients, colleagues, and the public, obtain consultation, and use the talents of other health professionals when indicated.

VI. A physician shall, in the provision of appropriate patient care, except in emergencies, be free to choose whom to serve, with whom to associate, and the environment in which to provide medical services.

VII. A physician shall recognize a responsibility to participate in activities contributing to an improved community.

3. American Nurses' Association Code for Nurses[3]

Preamble

Recipients and providers of nursing services are viewed as individuals and groups who possess basic rights and responsibilities, and whose values and circumstances command respect at all times. Nursing encompasses the promotion and restoration of health, the prevention of illness, and the alleviation of suffering. The statements of the Code and their interpretation provide guidance for conduct and relationships in carrying out nursing responsibilities consistent with the ethical obligations of the profession and quality in nursing care.

Code for Nurses

1. The nurse provides services with respect for human dignity and the uniqueness of the client unrestricted by considerations of social or economic status, personal attributes, or the nature of health problems.

2. The nurse safeguards the client's right to privacy by judiciously protecting information of a confidential nature.

3. The nurse acts to safeguard the client and the public when health care and safety are affected by the incompetent, unethical, or illegal practice of any person.

4. The nurse assumes responsibility and accountability for individual nursing judgments and actions.

5. The nurse maintains competence in nursing.

6. The nurse exercises informed judgment and uses individual competence and qualifications as criteria in seeking consultation, accepting responsibilities, and delegating nursing activities to others.

7. The nurse participates in activities that contribute to the ongoing development of the profession's body of knowledge.

8. The nurse participates in the profession's efforts to implement and improve standards of nursing.

9. The nurse participates in the profession's efforts to establish and maintain conditions of employment conducive to high-quality nursing care.

10. The nurse participates in the profession's effort to protect the public from misinformation and misrepresentation and to maintain the integrity of nursing.

11. The nurse collaborates with members of the health professions and other citizens in promoting community and national efforts to meet the health needs of the public.

4. American Psychological Association's Ethical Principles of Psychologists[4]

Preamble

Psychologists work to develop a valid and reliable body of scientific knowledge based on research. They may apply that knowledge to human behavior in a variety of contexts. In doing so, they perform many roles, such as researcher, educator, diagnostician, therapist, supervisor, consultant, administrator, social interventionist, and expert witness. Their goal is to broaden knowledge of behavior and, where appropriate, to apply it pragmatically to improve the condition of both the individual and society. Psychologists respect the central importance of freedom of inquiry and expression in research, teaching, and publication. They also strive to help the public in developing informed judgments and choices concerning human behavior. This Ethics Code provides a common set of values upon which psychologists build their professional and scientific work.

This Code is intended to provide both the general principles and the decision rules to cover most situations encountered by psychologists. It has as its primary goal the welfare and protection of the individuals and groups with whom psychologists work. It is the individual responsibility of each psychologist to aspire to the highest possible standards of conduct. Psychologists respect and protect human and civil rights, and do not knowingly participate in or condone unfair discriminatory practices.

The development of a dynamic set of ethical standards for a psychologist's work-related conduct requires a personal commitment to a lifelong effort to act ethically; to encourage ethical behavior by students, supervisees, employees, and colleagues, as appropriate; and to consult with others, as needed, concerning ethical problems. Each psychologist supplements, but does not violate, the Ethics Code's values and rules on the basis of guidance drawn from personal values, culture, and experience.

General Principles

Principle A: Competence

Psychologists strive to maintain high standards of competence in their work. They recognize the boundaries of their particular competencies and the limitations of their expertise. They provide only those services and use only those techniques for which they are qualified by education, training, or experience. Psychologists are cognizant of the fact that the competencies required in serving, teaching, and/or studying groups of people vary with the distinctive characteristics of those groups. In those areas in which recognized professional standards do not yet exist, psychologists exercise careful judgment and take appropriate precautions to protect the welfare of those with whom they work. They maintain knowledge of relevant scientific and professional information related to the services they render, and they recognize the need for ongoing education. Psychologists make appropriate use of scientific, professional, technical, and administrative resources.

Principle B: Integrity

Psychologists seek to promote integrity in the science, teaching, and practice of psychology. In these activities psychologists are honest, fair, and respectful of others. In describing or reporting their qualifications, services, products, fees, research, or teaching, they do not make statements that are false, misleading, or deceptive.

Psychologists strive to be aware of their own belief systems, values, needs, and limitations and the effect of these on their work. To the extent feasible, they attempt to clarify for relevant parties the roles they are performing and to function appropriately in accordance with those roles. Psychologists avoid improper and potentially harmful dual relationships.

Principle C: Professional and Scientific Responsibility

Psychologists uphold professional standards of conduct, clarify their professional roles and obligations, accept appropriate responsibility for their behavior, and adapt their methods to the needs of different populations. Psychologists consult with, refer to, or cooperate with other professionals and institutions to the extent needed to serve the best interests of their patients, clients, or other recipients of their services. Psychologists' moral standards and conduct are personal matters to the same degree as is true for any other person, except as psychologists' conduct may compromise their professional responsibilities or reduce the public's trust in psychology or psychologists. Psychologists are concerned about the ethical compliance of their colleagues' scientific and professional conduct. When appropriate, they consult with colleagues in order to prevent or avoid unethical conduct.

Principle D: Respect for People's Rights and Dignity

Psychologists accord appropriate respect to the fundamental rights, dignity, and worth of all people. They respect the rights of individuals to privacy, confidentiality, self-determination, and autonomy, mindful that legal and other obligations may lead to inconsistency and conflict with the exercise of these rights. Psychologists are aware of cultural, individual, and role differences, including those due to age, gender, race, ethnicity, national origin, religion, sexual orientation, disability, language, and socioeconomic status. Psychologists try to eliminate the effect on their work of biases based on those factors, and they do not knowingly participate in or condone unfair discriminatory practices.

Principle E: Concern for Others' Welfare

Psychologists seek to contribute to the welfare of those with whom they interact professionally. In their professional actions, psychologists weigh the welfare and rights of their patients or clients, students, supervisees, human research participants, and other affected persons, and the welfare of animal subjects of research. When conflicts occur among psychologists' obligations or concerns, they attempt to resolve these conflicts and to perform their roles in a responsible fashion that avoids or minimizes harm. Psychologists are sensitive to real and ascribed differences in power between themselves and others, and they do not exploit or mislead other people during or after professional relationships.

Principle F: Social Responsibility

Psychologists are aware of their professional and scientific responsibilities to the community and the society in which they work and live. They apply and make public their knowledge of psychology in order to contribute to human welfare. Psychologists are concerned about and work to mitigate the causes of human suffering. When undertaking research, they strive to advance human welfare and the science of psychology. Psychologists try to avoid misuse of their work. Psychologists comply with the law and encourage the development of law and social policy that serve the interests of their patients and clients and the public. They are encouraged to contribute a portion of their professional time for little or no personal advantage.

5. The Nuremberg Code[5]

1. The voluntary consent of the human subject is absolutely essential.

This means that the person involved should have legal capacity to give consent; should be so situated as to be able to exercise free power of choice, without the intervention of any element of force, fraud, deceit, duress, over-reaching, or other ulterior form of constraint or coercion; and should have sufficient knowledge and comprehension of the elements of the subject matter involved as to enable him to make an understanding and enlightened decision. This latter element requires that before the acceptance of an affirmative decision by the experimental subject there should be made known to him the nature, duration, and purpose of the experiment; the method and means by which it is to be conducted; all inconveniences and hazards reasonably to be expected; and the effects upon his health or person which may possibly come from his participation in the experiment.

The duty and responsibility for ascertaining the quality of the consent rests upon each individual who initiates, directs, or engages in the experiment. It is a personal duty and responsibility which may not be delegated to another with impunity.

2. The experiment should be such as to yield fruitful results for the good of society, unprocurable by other methods or means of study, and not random and unnecessary in nature.

3. The experiment should be so designed and based on the results of animal experimentation and a knowledge of the natural history of the disease or other problem under study that the anticipated results will justify the performance of the experiment.

4. The experiment should be so conducted as to avoid all unnecessary physical and mental suffering and injury.

5. No experiment should be conducted where there is an *a priori* reason to believe that death or disabling injury will occur; except, perhaps, in those experiments where the experimental physicians also serve as subjects.

6. The degree of risk to be taken should never exceed that determined by the humanitarian importance of the problem to be solved by the experiment.

7. Proper preparations should be made and adequate facilities provided to protect the experimental subject against even remote possibilities of injury, disability, or death.

8. The experiment should be conducted only by scientifically qualified persons. The highest degree of skill and care should be required through all stages of the experiment of those who conduct or engage in the experiment.

9. During the course of the experiment the human subject should be at liberty to bring the experiment to an end if he has reached the physical or mental state where continuation of the experiment seems to him to be impossible.

10. During the course of the experiment the scientist in charge must be prepared to terminate the experiment at any stage, if he has probable cause to believe, in the exercise of the good faith, superior skill, and careful judgment required of him that a continuation of the experiment is likely to result in injury, disability, or death to the experimental subject.

6. Code of Ethics for Engineers[6]
Accreditation Board for Engineering and Technology

The Fundamental Principles

Engineers uphold and advance the integrity, honor and dignity of the engineering profession by:

I. using their knowledge and skill for the enhancement of human welfare;

II. being honest and impartial, and serving with fidelity the public, their employers and clients;

III. striving to increase the competence and prestige of the engineering profession; and

IV. supporting the professional and technical societies of their disciplines.

The Fundamental Canons

1. Engineers shall hold paramount the safety, health and welfare of the public in the performance of their professional duties.

2. Engineers shall perform services only in the areas of their competence.

3. Engineers shall issue public statements only in an objective and truthful manner.

4. Engineers shall act in professional matters for each employer or client as faithful agents or trustees, and shall avoid conflicts of interest.

5. Engineers shall build their professional reputation on the merit of their services and shall not compete unfairly with others.

6. Engineers shall act in such a manner as to uphold and enhance the honor, integrity and dignity of the profession.

7. Engineers shall continue their professional development throughout their careers and shall provide opportunities for the professional development of those engineers under their supervision.

7. Code of Ethics for Engineers[7]
National Society of Professional Engineers

Preamble

Engineering is an important and learned profession. The members of the profession recognize that their work has a direct and vital impact on the quality of life for all people. Accordingly, the services provided by engineers require honesty, impartiality fairness and equity, and must be dedicated to the protection of the public health, safety and welfare. In the practice of their profession, engineers must perform under a standard of professional behavior which requires adherence to the highest principles of ethical conduct on behalf of the public, clients, employers and the profession.

I. Fundamental Canons

Engineers, in the fulfillment of their professional duties, shall:

1. Hold paramount the safety, health and welfare of the public in the performance of their professional duties.

2. Perform services only in areas of their competence.

3. Issue public statements only in an objective and truthful manner.

4. Act in professional matters for each employer or client as faithful agents or trustees

5. Avoid deceptive acts in the solicitation of professional employment.

II. Rules of Practice

1. Engineers shall hold paramount the safety, health and welfare of the public in the performance of their professional duties.

2. Engineers shall perform services only in the areas of their competence.

3. Engineers shall issue public statements only in an objective and truthful manner.

4. Engineers shall act in professional matters for each employer or client as faithful agents or trustees.

5. Engineers shall avoid deceptive acts in the solicitation of professional employment.

III. Professional Obligations

1. Engineers shall be guided in all their professional relations by the highest standards of integrity.

2. Engineers shall at all times strive to serve the public interest.

3. Engineers shall avoid all conduct or practice which is likely to discredit the profession or deceive the public.

4. Engineers shall not disclose confidential information concerning the business affairs or technical processes of any present or former client or employer without his consent.

5. Engineers shall not be influenced in their professional duties by conflicting interests.

6. Engineers shall uphold the principle of appropriate and adequate compensation for those engaged in engineering work.

7. Engineers shall not attempt to obtain employment or advancement or professional engagements by untruthfully criticizing other engineers, or by other improper or questionable methods.

8. Engineers shall not attempt to injure, maliciously or falsely, directly or indirectly, the professional reputation, prospects, practice or employment of other engineers, nor untruthfully criticize other engineers' work. Engineers who believe others are guilty of unethical or illegal practice shall present such information to the proper authority for action.

9. Engineers shall accept responsibility for their professional activities; provided, however, that Engineers may seek indemnification for professional services arising out of their practice for other than gross negligence, where the Engineer's interests cannot otherwise be protected.

10. Engineers shall give credit for engineering work to those to whom credit is due and will recognize the proprietary interests of others.

11. Engineers shall cooperate in extending the effectiveness of the profession by interchanging information and experience with other engineers and students, and will endeavor to provide opportunity for the professional development and advancement of engineers under their supervision.

8. American Bar Association's Model Rules of Professional Conduct (Preamble)[8]

Preamble: A Lawyer's Responsibilities

A lawyer is a representative of clients, an officer of the legal system and a public citizen having special responsibility for the quality of justice.

As a representative of clients, a lawyer performs various functions. As advisor, a lawyer provides a client with an informed understanding of the client's legal rights and obligations and explains their practical implications. As advocate, a lawyer zealously asserts the client's position under the rules of the adversary system. As negotiator, a lawyer seeks a result advantageous to the client but consistent with requirements of honest dealing with others. As intermediary between clients, a lawyer seeks to reconcile their divergent interests as an advisor and, to a limited extent, as a spokesperson for each client. A lawyer acts as evaluator by examining a client's legal affairs and reporting about them to the client or to others.

In all professional functions a lawyer should be competent, prompt and diligent. A lawyer should maintain communication with a client concerning the representation. A lawyer should keep in confidence information relating to representation of a client except so far as disclosure is required or permitted by the Rules of Professional Conduct or other law.

A lawyer's conduct should conform to the requirements of the law, both in professional service to clients and in the lawyer's business and personal affairs. A lawyer should use the law's procedures only for legitimate purposes and not to harass or intimidate others. A lawyer should demonstrate respect for the legal system and for those who serve it, including judges, other lawyers and public officials. While it is a lawyer's duty, when necessary, to challenge the rectitude of official action, it is also a lawyer's duty to uphold legal process.

As a public citizen, a lawyer should seek improvement of the law, the administration of justice and the quality of service rendered by the legal profession. As a member of a learned profession, a lawyer should cultivate knowledge of the law beyond its use for clients, employ that knowledge in reform of the law and work to strengthen legal education.

A lawyer should be mindful of deficiencies in the administration of justice and of the fact that the poor, and sometimes persons who are not poor, cannot afford adequate legal assistance, and should therefore devote professional time and civic influence in their behalf. A lawyer should aid the legal profession in pursuing these objectives and should help the bar regulate itself in the public interest.

Many of a lawyer's professional responsibilities are prescribed in the Rules of Professional Conduct, as well as substantive and procedural law. However, a lawyer is also guided by personal conscience and the approbation of professional peers. A lawyer should strive to attain the highest level of skill, to improve the law and the legal profession and to exemplify the legal profession's ideals of public service.

A lawyer's responsibilities as a representative of clients, an officer of the legal system and a public citizen are usually harmonious. Thus, when an opposing party is well represented, a lawyer can be a zealous advocate on behalf of a client and at the same time assume that justice is being done. So also, a lawyer can be sure that preserving client confidences ordinarily serves the public interest because people are more likely to seek legal advice, and thereby heed their legal obligations, when they know their communications will be private.

In the nature of law practice, however, conflicting responsibilities are encountered. Virtually all difficult ethical problems arise from conflict between a lawyer's responsibilities to clients, to the legal system and to the lawyer's own interest in remaining an upright person while earning a satisfactory living. The Rules of Professional Conduct prescribe terms for resolving such conflicts. Within the framework of these Rules, many difficult issues of professional discretion can arise. Such issues must be resolved through the exercise of sensitive professional and moral judgment guided by the basic principles underlying the Rules.

The legal profession is largely self-governing. Although other professions also have been granted powers of self-government, the legal profession is unique in this respect because of the close relationship between the profession and the processes of government and law enforcement. This connection is manifested in the fact that ultimate authority over the legal profession is vested largely in the courts.

To the extent that lawyers meet the obligations of their professional calling, the occasion for government regulation is obviated. Self-regulation also helps maintain the legal profession's independence from government domination. An independent legal profession is an important force in preserving government under law, for abuse of legal authority is more readily challenged by a profession whose members are not dependent on government for the right to practice.

The legal profession's relative autonomy carries with it special responsibilities of self-government. The profession has a responsibility to assure that its regulations are conceived in the public interest and not in furtherance of parochial or self-interested concerns of the bar. Every lawyer is responsible for observance of the Rules of Professional Conduct. A lawyer should also aid in securing their observance by other lawyers. Neglect of these responsibilities compromises the independence of the profession and the public interest which it serves.

Lawyers play a vital role in the preservation of society. The fulfillment of this role requires an understanding by lawyers of their relationship to our legal system. The Rules of Professional Conduct, when properly applied, serve to define that relationship.

9. Standards of Ethical Conduct for Management Accountants[9]

Management accountants have an obligation to the organizations they serve, their profession, the public, and themselves to maintain the highest standards of ethical conduct. In recognition of this obligation, the National Association of Accountants has promulgated the following standards of ethical conduct for management accountants. Adherence to these standards is integral to achieving the *Objectives of Management Accounting*. Management accountants shall not commit acts contrary to these standards nor shall they condone the commission of such acts by others within their organizations.

Competence

Management accountants have a responsibility to:

- Maintain an appropriate level of professional competence by ongoing development of their knowledge and skills.
- Perform their professional duties in accordance with relevant laws, regulations, and technical standards.

- Prepare complete and clear reports and recommendations after appropriate analyses of relevant and reliable information.

Confidentiality

Management accountants have a responsibility to:

- Refrain from disclosing confidential information acquired in the course of their work except when authorized, unless legally obligated to do so.

- Inform subordinates as appropriate regarding the confidentiality of information acquired in the course of their work and monitor their activities to assure the maintenance of that confidentiality.

- Refrain from using or appearing to use confidential information acquired in the course of their work for unethical or illegal advantage either personally or through third parties.

Integrity

Management accountants have a responsibility to:

- Avoid actual or apparent conflicts of interest and advise all appropriate parties of any potential conflict.

- Refrain from engaging in any activity that would prejudice their ability to carry out their duties ethically.

- Refuse any gift, favor, or hospitality that would influence or would appear to influence their actions.

- Refrain from either actively or passively subverting the attainment of the organization's legitimate and ethical objectives.

- Recognize and communicate professional limitations or other constraints that would preclude responsible judgment or successful performance of an activity.

- Communicate unfavorable as well as favorable information and professional judgments or opinions.

- Refrain from engaging in or supporting any activity that would discredit the profession.

Objectivity

Management accountants have a responsibility to:

- Communicate information fairly and objectively.

- Disclose fully all relevant information that could reasonably be expected to influence an intended user's understanding of the reports, comments, and recommendations presented.

Resolution of Ethical Conflict

In applying the standards of ethical conduct, management accountants may encounter problems in identifying unethical behavior or in resolving an ethical conflict. When faced with significant ethical issues, management accountants should follow the established policies of the organization bearing on the resolution of such conflict. If these policies do not resolve the ethical conflict, management accountants should consider the following courses of action:

- Discuss such problems with the immediate superior except when it appears that the superior is involved, in which case the problem should be presented initially to the next higher managerial level. If satisfactory resolution cannot be achieved when the problem is initially presented, submit the issues to the next higher managerial level.

  If the immediate superior is the chief executive officer, or equivalent, the acceptable reviewing authority may be a group such as the audit committee, executive committee, board of directors, board of trustees, or owners. Contact with levels above the immediate superior should be initiated only with the superior's knowledge, assuming the superior is not involved.

- Clarify relevant concepts by confidential discussion with an objective advisor to obtain an understanding of possible courses of action.

- If the ethical conflict still exists after exhausting all levels of internal review, the management accountant may have no other recourse on significant matters than to resign from the organization and to submit an informative memorandum to an appropriate representative of the organization.

Except where legally prescribed, communication of such problems to authorities or individuals not employed or engaged by the organization is not considered appropriate.

10. Code of Ethics of Financial Executives Institute[10]

To be eligible for active membership in Financial Executives Institute, applicants must possess those personal attributes such as character, personal integrity and business ability that will be an asset to the Institute. They must also meet preestablished criteria indicating a high degree of participation in the formulation of policies for the operation of the enterprises they represent and in the administration of the financial functions. Members of the Institute are expected to follow this Code of Ethics.

As a member of Financial Executives Institute, I will:

- Conduct my business and personal affairs at all times with honesty and integrity.

- Provide complete, appropriate and relevant information in an objective manner when reporting to management, stockholders, employees, government agencies, other institutions and the public.

- Comply with rules and regulations of federal, state, provincial, and local governments, and other appropriate private and public regulatory agencies.

- Discharge duties and responsibilities to my employer to the best of my ability, including complete communication on all matters within my jurisdiction.

- Maintain the confidentiality of information acquired in the course of my work except when authorized or otherwise legally obligated to disclose. Confidential information acquired in the course of my work will not be used for my personal advantage.

- Maintain an appropriate level of professional competence through continuing development of my knowledge and skills.

- Refrain from committing acts discreditable to myself, my employer, FEI or fellow members of the Institute.

Notes to Appendix One

1. Owsei Temkin and C. Lilian Temkin, eds. *Ancient Medicine: Selected Papers of Ludwig Edelstein*. (Baltimore: The Johns Hopkins University Press, 1967), p. 6.

2. Copyright © 1982, 1983, 1984, 1986, 1989, 1992 by the American Medical Association. All rights reserved. Reprinted with permission of the American Medical Association.

3. Reprinted with permission from *Code for Nurses with Interpretive Statements*, © 1985, American Nurses Association, Washington, D.C.

4. Ethical Principles of Psychologists and Code of Conduct, *American Psychologist,* December 1992. Copyright 1992 by the American Psychological Association. Reprinted by permission.

5. *Trials of War Criminals Before the Nuremberg Military Tribunals*. (Washington D.C.: U.S. Government Printing Office, 1948).

6. Reprinted with permission from the Accreditation Board for Engineering and Technology.

7. Reprinted with permission from the National Society of Professional Engineers. NSPE Publication No. 1102 as revised January 1990. We have abridged the Rules of Conduct and Professional Obligations by including each main section but omitting the subsections pertaining to each.

8. Center for Professional Responsibility, American Bar Association, copyright 1992. Copies of the ABA Model Rules of Professional Conduct are available from Order Fulfillment, American Bar Association, 750 North Lake Shore Drive, Chicago, IL 60611.

9. The Standards of Ethical Conduct for Management Accountants is reprinted with permission of the Institute of Management Accountants.

10. Copyright by the Financial Executives Institute, 10 Madison Avenue, P.O. Box 1938, Morristown, New Jersey 07962-1938.

Appendix 2

How to Write a Case Study Report

In this appendix, we offer directions for writing a case study report in applied professional ethics. We have found that such reports are good exercises for students in professional programs. They demand the same kind of careful thinking expected in academic papers, though they are more similar to reports that professionals will write during their careers than to the kinds of papers that many academics write and assign.

These directions will work best when applied to "hard cases," that is, cases involving a moral dilemma. Some cases, however, may not require the same kind of analysis that we suggest. For example, if you are studying a case that is primarily an example of moral heroism, then these directions may not precisely fit. In these cases, the point is often to learn from the example of others. In most applied ethics cases, on the other hand, there will be a central dilemma that needs to be resolved. The point in these cases is to give you practice in moral decision making. For cases that contain a moral dilemma, the following directions should help.

1. How to Research the Case.

A. Gather Background Material.

Before you begin writing a case study report in professional ethics, you should research the case as thoroughly as possible. This might include studying the history, legal aspects and any other relevant facts surrounding the case. Since an ethical analysis can only occur after you have familiarized yourself with the case, start with good research.

For a variety of reasons, it may not be possible to have a complete knowledge of the case, but you should find out as much as you can.

B. Analyze the Case.

During the research stage, you can begin to ask analytical questions. To analyze means to take something apart. During your moral analysis of the case, you should take apart the case, sifting out potential problems. Problems and disagreements often arise in three areas. First, there are sometimes factual problems. Will this medication cure these symptoms in a person of this age? Is this structure safe in these weather conditions? Did that person intend what others have said, or was it an accident? Second, there are sometimes conceptual problems. It is important to clearly define what you and others mean, because disagreements are often based on differences in definition rather than matters of moral principle. Finally, there may be problems in the area of ethics.

Don't confuse factual or conceptual problems with moral problems. Insofar as you can, matters of fact and conceptual issues should be addressed before your moral analysis. Disagreements about the facts should be resolved with a method appropriate to the subject matter. Medical questions should be answered by those qualified to do so and using a method appropriate to the problem. The same is true if the disagreement is a technical one in any area. Conceptual difficulties may be philosophical in nature, but that does not mean that their resolution is based on a moral principle. They should be resolved through careful thinking. Be careful though, because moral judgments often depend on how you define things, and what you accept as a fact.

Disagreements about the moral issues of the case may be affected by the level of moral judgment of those involved in the case. Further, others who are studying the case may focus on different moral issues, depending on their own level of moral judgment. As a professional, you should be able to understand the self-interested perspective of Level One, or the convention-maintaining perspective of Level Two, though you should ultimately evaluate the case from the Level Three perspective of respect for persons.

C. Evaluate the Case.

To evaluate the case, after you have analyzed the case and determined the main moral problem, you should apply the principles set forth in Chapter Four. You should be able to determine whether a given action treats others with respect. To apply the moral principles, you should focus on the intention, motive and circumstances, as discussed in Chapter Five.

Throughout your research, you should remain open to further dialogue, since your analysis and evaluation may affect your understanding of the facts of the case and the need for a deeper understanding of the case. Being open to further dialogue will also allow you to remember that the case may change and develop over time.

2. How to Write the Case Report.

Divide your work into clear sections. Your report will show clearer thinking and better writing if you divide your report into several sections. We recommend the following format, though we recognize that some cases may be better presented by an alternate approach, or by emphasizing one or the other of the sections that we recommend.

A. Background.

In this section, you should explain the relevant history and background of the case. The length of this section will vary depending on the nature of the case that you are studying and the nature of your assignment.

B. Statement of the Problem.

This section will likely be the shortest section of your report, though the thinking involved may take the most effort. It will help to frame the problem by looking at the conflicting interests, roles and principles involved in the case. Once you have identified the problem, state it clearly and concisely. If there is more than one problem, make that clear.

C. Analysis.

The analysis should separate out factual and conceptual issues so that you can focus on the moral issues involved in the case. Your analysis will be aided by looking at the case from Level One, Level Two and Level Three. In the end, all of these perspectives should be brought together and balanced. The lower levels should be subordinated to the higher. However, in your analysis, it will help to focus on each individually. It may help to make explicit what moral principles apply (using Chapter Four) and how they apply (using Chapter Five).

D. Possible Solutions.

In this section, you should state the different courses of action available. For example, a certain alternative may appear desirable from the Level One perspective of self-interest. Yet from Level Two, that choice may seem socially inappropriate. Further, from the Level Three perspective, it may be impermissible if it is contrary to moral principle. So this section should briefly list possible courses of action and briefly state the advantages and disadvantages of each.

E. Recommended Course of Action.

After you have set forth and explained various possible alternatives, you should recommend a course of action. State why that course of action is morally desirable. Take into account the moral principles explained in Chapter Three. Measure the intention and motive against those principles. Show how the circumstances warrant the action. Consider the relationships involved. Finally, use sound reasoning to defend your recommended course of action.

F. Steps for Implementation.

Show how your recommended course of action should be implemented. It is here that circumstances are most relevant. A consideration of the concrete circumstances will help to determine what steps to take in order to apply the principle of respect. You might consider both how to resolve this case and how to avoid similar problems in the future.

3. Concluding Remarks.

Of course not every case lends itself to this precise outline. In some cases, the analysis and possible solutions may be done together. Sometimes, it may help to distinguish between short term and long term solutions by adding a separate section for each. Still, an outline similar to the one suggested here will give structure to your case study report.

Appendix 3

Examples of Student Case Study Reports

This medical ethics case study report was written by a nursing student and is based on an actual case at the hospital where the student worked.

To Code or Not to Code:
A Case Study in Nursing Ethics

A. Background

"Liz" is a 57 year old woman admitted to the hospital because she fainted in a shopping mall. An EKG that was done showed that she had some cardia arrhythmias that may have caused her to faint. During her stay in the hospital, she was being given medications for her heart and her heart rhythm was being monitored 24 hours a day. One evening the R.N. taking care of Liz noticed on the heart monitor that she was having an increased number of arrhythmias. The nurse looked at her patient's chart and saw that her advance directives indicated that Liz did not want to be resuscitated should her condition get worse. When the nurse entered the room, she saw Liz scared and pale. While the nurse was assessing the situation, Liz told her that she could feel something was wrong and she wasn't ready to die. She told the R.N. that she wanted everything done to save her. Just after saying this, Liz went into cardiac arrest.When this happened, the nurse had a difficult decision to make. The R.N. decided to follow Liz's verbal wishes and she immediately called a code. The doctors, nurses and resuscitation team were successful and Liz's heart began beating and she was transferred to the critical care unit. When the nurse notified the family of what had happened, the family was upset that Liz was resuscitated when the advance directives said not to. Once the family found out that Liz had told the nurse otherwise just before she coded, they questioned Liz's state of mind when she said that. As this is being written, Liz is still in the critical care unit. She remains on medication and needs a lot of care, but she is making progress. The family is sympathetic with the nurse. They understand her dilemma and are not taking legal actions. However it is questionable how things would have turned out if Liz's condition was worse.

B. Statement of the Problem

The problem in this case is whether or not the nurse should call a code. The advance directives, agreed to by the patient, said that the patient should not be resuscitated. The patient made a verbal request that contradicted the advance directive, stating that "she wanted everything done to save her." Should the nurse follow the advance directive or the verbal request?

C. Analysis and Possible Solutions

This case looks different when viewed from each of Kohlberg's three levels. If the nurse acted from Level One, the primary concern would be to protect her job and to avoid legal liability. She would most likely follow the advance directive so that the decision would not depend on her.

If the nurse acted from Level Two, the primary concern would be to conform to the expectations for her behavior. Most likely, a Level Two response would be to conform to the expectations of the advance directive. She might be concerned with the reputation of the nursing staff and the hospital. However, she also has an institutional role to act on behalf of the patient, and that may mean follow the verbal request. So even at Level Two, it is a complicated case. She has to weigh two competing pressures. One is her role as the patient's advocate. The other is her role as an employee of the hospital. Her decision might open the hospital to legal action. If she decided to call a code and the patient ended up in a coma, the hospital would likely have been sued. Consequently, even though it is not a clear case when analyzed from this perspective, the most likely Level Two response would be to follow the advance directive.

If the nurse acted from Level Three, the guiding principle would be respect for persons. The principle of respect for persons recognizes the ability of individuals to make their own free decisions. The difficulty in this case is that the nurse must make an assessment of Liz's state of mind when she made her verbal request.

The nurse's intention of calling a code conformed to the principle of respect since the nurse aimed to respect the patient's wishes. The motive was to save her life. There are a number of circumstances that are relevant to the case. Her age needs to be taken into consideration, as well as the prospects for recovery. Liz was 57 years old, and the nurse made a professional judgment that the verbal request was sincere. Another consideration is the timing of the request. The verbal request almost immediately preceded the onset of the cardiac arrest. There was no time to change the directive. Also, the nurse was present during the onset of the cardiac arrest, so that resuscitation could begin immediately with a greater chance of success.

Another principle that comes into effect is the principle of integrity. This applies to the R.N. As a professional nurse, it is her responsibility to be a patient advocate. Although there were no other witnesses to hear Liz's request, the nurse felt an obligation to respect Liz's wishes.

From the perspective of Level Three, the nurse treated Liz with the respect befitting a person rather than simply conforming to the rules expressed in the advance directive.

D. Recommended Course of Action

In this case, I agree with the course of action taken by the nurse. Legally, what the nurse did was risky because a lawsuit might have been brought against the hospital if the situation had not turned out as well as it did. The nurse did what she thought she had to do to help the patient.

This was a difficult situation that was handled quickly and turned out to everyone's approval. The nurse feels she acted responsibly, maintained the standards for being a professional nurse and made a professional decision.

This paper was written in a "Business and Applied Ethics" course by an engineering student.

The 1970 Ground Testing Incident of the DC-10

This report examines one chapter in the history of the DC-10. While the DC-10 has been involved in several major crashes, including one in 1979 in Chicago and another in 1989 in Sioux City, the 1970 ground test relates most directly to the 1974 Paris crash in which 346 lives were lost.

BACKGROUND:

Early in 1968, McDonnell Douglas sent out a Subcontractor Bid Document which outlined Douglas's requirements for the design of the DC-10's fuselage and doors to five competing aerospace companies, including Convair division of General Dynamics, North American Rockwell, Rohr Aircraft, and Aerfer.[1] On August 7, 1968 McDonnell Douglas signed a subcontract with Convair division of General Dynamics. William Gross of McDonnell Douglas later said that Convair was chosen based both on the sound financial background of its mother company and upon the company's outstanding record in structural design. Focus upon the design of the aircraft's doors was brought about early on primarily due to Douglas's decision to route hydraulic and control cables for the aircraft's aft engine and horizontal stabilizer through the floor beams that separated the passenger compartment and the cargo bay. This design put these control mechanisms in great danger of being damaged in the event of sudden decompression during high altitude flight. If decompression occurred at altitudes above roughly 12,000 feet, the floor would likely fail and buckle, thus damaging the hydraulic and control cables greatly reducing or possibly preventing the crews ability to fly the airplane. (This is precisely what happened in the 1974 Parish Crash).

In the original Subcontractor Bid Document, Douglas requirements called for plug type design of the passenger doors and outward hinging tension-latch lower cargo doors. The plug design for the passenger doors is based upon a door that is hinged to open to the inside of the airplane therefore pressurization of the airplane only serves to tighten the seal of the door. The problem existed with the lower cargo doors which open to the outside of the plane. Therefore they rely heavily on the latch and locking system to prevent them from opening during flight. Douglas's original requirements were based upon the use of over-center latches driven by hydraulic cylinders, a system that had already been used on some DC-8 and DC-9 doors. As an extra precaution, the original design was to have a manual locking system designed so that the handle or latch lever could not be stowed unless the door was properly closed and latched.

In November of 1968 Douglas told Convair engineers that they must use electric actuators rather than the original hydraulic actuators. Douglas stated that the change in design would save 28 pounds of weight per door and that the new design would conform to airline practice. However this new design that made use of electric rather than hydraulic actuators made the need for a fail-safe locking mechanism even more important. The original hydraulic actuator system was a more positive design, for in the event that the latch failed to lock properly as the plane began its climb, it would force the hydraulic cylinders to reverse, thus opening the door and allowing depressurization of the cargo bay. Unlike the electric actuators, this would occur gradually and at a lower altitude where the cabin floor could still sustain the pressure differential acting upon it without any buckling.

In August of 1969 Convair submitted, per request of McDonnell Douglas, a draft FMEA (Failure Mode and Effects Analysis) report to the contracting company in order to meet the FAA requirement that an FMEA must be given for all major systems that are critical to safety. Although based on an early design, Convair was very critical as to the safety of the lower cargo door as designed. First Convair stressed that no great reliance should be put upon warning lights that would be placed on the flight deck because failures in the indicator circuits would not likely be discovered during preflight checks. Convair also stressed the point that it would be very difficult for ground crews to determine whether the latching system had locked properly based solely on visual inspection of the handle location. The draft FMEA went on to describe nine possible failure sequences which could lead to a hazard involving danger to life. Five of these involved danger to ground crew from a door suddenly falling shut or open unrelated to the in flight problem of rapid depressurization. One of these addressed a failure of the locking pin system due to jamming of the locking tube or one or more of the locking pins themselves. In this case the indicator light would indicate a door locked position while in reality a malfunction in the electric actuators would result in the unlocked doors opening in flight. The FMEA went on to predict that the results of this case would be rapid depressurization and possibly structural failure of the floor. The other three cases described possibilities of total latch failure due to electrical faults with the door being held shut only by the electrical system that was intended to close the door. Overall the draft FMEA showed Convair's mistrust of the early design and the dangers involved in the bad design of the latch and locking mechanism on the lower cargo doors.

As lead manufacturer, Douglas took on the responsibility for the certification of the airplane and chose not to show Convair's draft FMEA or any other report that pointed out the dangers of the lower cargo doors to the FAA. In fact, under the terms of the subcontract, McDonnell Douglas had forbidden Convair from directly contacting the FAA about the DC-10.

On May 29, 1970 during a ground test of the first DC-10's air conditioning system, Convair engineers' predictions became a reality. In order to test the air conditioning system a pressure differential of four to five pounds per square inch had to be built up inside the hull. Suddenly the forward lower cargo door blew open resulting in a large section of the cabin floor collapsing into the cargo bay. Although Douglas did admit that some modification of the cargo doors would be necessary before FAA certification, they blamed the incident on human failure of the mechanic who had closed the door, not on the latch and locking system of the door.

In response to the ground testing incident, Douglas decided to replace the spring loaded locking system with a hand driven system in which a small plug type vent door would be located to the right of the handle used to move the locking pins into position. In theory the vent door would not close unless the locking pins were in the locked position. Although intended to do so, the vent door system added very little safety to the cargo door latch-lock system as designed. Douglas's design placed the vent door on a separate torque tube than the tube that actually drove the locking pins into place. The two separate tubes were interconnected only by adjustable linkages which if improperly adjusted or perhaps even missing would mean that the vent door could close without the locking pins being properly in place. It was also discovered that the linkages had not undergone the proper stress testing and that under a certain amount of stress the linkages would bend. This bending would allow the vent door to close, indicating a locked position, when in actuality it was not locked.

In theory this flawed vent door system should have never passed FAA certification, but the way the certification procedure is structured required that much of the certification testing was done by Douglas's own engineers who had been appointed by the FAA to serve as DER's (Designated Engineering Representatives). In the case of the DC-10, the FAA carried out only 11,055 of the 42,950 inspections required to meet the federal air worthiness regulations that must be met prior to certification of the airplane. In the case of the vent door design, the same man who approved the testing conducted by McDonnell Douglas itself also served as the FAA's DER and approved the report of the tests as having passed the required federal air worthiness regulations.

It should be noted that not everyone on the design team was satisfied with the safety the vent door design provided. In November 1970, a Convair engineer named H.B. Riggs wrote an internal memo addressing how he felt the problem could have been better handled. In the memorandum Riggs stated that the conceptual design of the vent door provided by Douglas was less than desirable and went further to address the following possible solutions: going back to hydraulic actuation; adding redundant electric circuits as back-up on the electric actuators; interlinking the door closing system with the pressurization system; increasing the floor strength sufficiently to make the floor resist any possible pressure differential after a door blowout; providing vent space in the floor to enable high-pressure air to escape without doing damage. None of Riggs suggestions were ever incorporated on the DC-10 and were never mentioned to FAA inspectors during certification of the airplane.

In January of 1971, with only seven months to go before the scheduled certification date of the DC-10, Douglas ordered that the vent doors as designed be placed on all lower cargo doors. In addition Douglas maintained that since the passenger floor which was designed and constructed to meet Douglas specifications under the Convair subcontract had failed during the 1970 ground test, they believed that Convair should bear the financial burden of installing the vent doors as a safety precaution. On July 29, 1971 the DC-10 was certified by the FAA with the Douglas designed vent doors in place despite the subcontractors lack of faith in the system.

STATEMENT OF THE PROBLEM:

The primary problem in this case lies in the failure on the part of both McDonnell Douglas and their subcontractor, Convair division of General Dynamics, to realize and act upon their duty to produce a safe product. A second problem also exists in the FAA procedure that allowed a engineer, employed by the manufacturer, to approve a test report that was constructed and signed under his authority.

POSSIBLE SOLUTIONS:

Since there are two main problems in this case, two sets of solutions will be offered.

Possible Technical Solutions:

1) Use the vent door system as designed.

2) Return to the use of hydraulically driven actuators rather than electrically driven actuators.

3) Add redundant electric circuits as backups on the electric actuators.

4) Interlink the door closing system to the pressurization system.

5) Increase floor strength sufficiently to make the floor capable of withstanding possible pressure differentials experienced in the event of a door blowout.

6) Provide vent space in the floor to enable high-pressure air to escape without damaging the floor.

7) Redesign the vent door design so that closure of the vent door is directly dependent upon proper positioning of the locking pins rather than just being coincidental to it.

Possible Preventive Solutions:

1) Continue the current relationship between the manufacturer and the FAA that places the role of the inspector in the hands of employees of the manufacturer.

2) Establishment of a safety board to oversee all safety test results, board should consist both of engineers employed by the manufacturer and by FAA employed inspectors.

RECOMMENDED SOLUTIONS:

My first recommendation to McDonnell Douglas and the subcontractor Convair would be to stress the importance and the responsibility they have to the general public to produce a safe product. This recommendation requires that the employees and management of the two companies have an understanding as to what a safe product is. The obligation to produce a safe product flows from the principles of respect and non-malevolence.

Safety is not an absolute concept. For example, here is no such thing as an absolutely safe airplane. Still, some airplanes are safer than others, and it is possible to articulate the reasons why one aircraft is safer than another. In light of this, I suggest the following definition of safety:

> A thing is safe (to a certain degree) with respect to a given person or group at a given time if, were they fully aware of its risks and expressing their most settled values, they would judge those risks to be acceptable (to a certain degree).[2]

It seems clear to me through Convair's draft FMEA and later intercompany memorandums that engineers working on the project recognized that the latch-lock design of the cargo doors represented, at a minimum, questionable safety standards. If passengers were aware of the problems with the door and its relation to the cables under the floor, they would likely deem the aircraft unsafe. It was here, where their efforts to meet scheduling deadlines and in their efforts to keep costs to a minimum, the two companies failed to act on the principle of non-malevolence that would have forbidden them from making decisions that could possibly pose a danger to the people who would later be flying on their airplane.

My second recommendation depends on the first, in that when Douglas and Convair recognized the cargo doors as a safety problem, the principle of non-malevolence would have required them to formulate an effective technical solution that would have eliminated the unnecessary dangers associated with the latch-lock system used on the lower cargo doors. Keeping in mind their duty to produce a safe product and their obligation to produce a sellable product, the companies should have determined which one of the possible solutions was best. My recommendation would be to redesign the vent door system in order to make the closing of the vent door directly dependent upon the proper positioning of the locking pins. This could most easily be done by eliminating the weak adjustable linkages currently used, and driving the locking pins into place using the same torque tube that would close the vent door itself.

My second suggestion would be to employ some venting in the passenger floor as a backup precaution that would allow high pressure air to escape without buckling the floor in the event of rapid depressurization.

These modifications would ensure the safety of the passengers at the least cost to the manufacturer and maintain the airplane's marketability to the airlines who want a safe, dependable, and easily maintainable aircraft.

After resolving the immediate safety problems, it seems imperative that the relationship between the manufacturers and the FAA that allowed such a poor design to be certified as a safe aircraft needs to be reworked. My suggestion would be to establish a safety board, consisting of two members who are engineers employed by the manufacturer, and two other members who would be FAA inspectors. In this manner both the company's manufacturing interests and the FAA's regulatory interests would be represented, while eliminating the conflict of roles that an FAA appointed DER faces between one's role as an employee of the manufacturer and one's role as an FAA inspector. Under this system, all safety tests would be reviewed by this safety board, and if any questions arose, the company's test engineers could be called in to justify or explain the test results and the implications that they might have on safety. The board would be required to come to a unanimous decision in order to grant approval of any safety inspection, and would be signed by all four members of the safety board. The safety board should also be made available to any employee of the company or the subcontracting companies who wishes to report, anonymously if the person so desires, what he or she may consider to be a safety problem. I feel that this structure would greater ensure the FAA's ability to govern federal air worthiness regulations, and force the manufacturer and its subcontractor to take more responsibility to ensure that they are producing a safe product.

Notes

1. Much of the background material for this report is taken from Paul Eddy, et. al, "The 1970 Ground Testing Incident" in *The DC-10 Case: A Study in Applied Ethics, Technology and Society*. Ed. Fielder & Birsch. (Albany: SUNY Press, 1992), pp. 83-91.

2. Mike W. Martin and Ronald Schinzinger, *Ethics and Engineering*. (New York: McGraw-Hill, 1983) p. 97.

Appendix 4

Some Works on Moral Theory

Students of applied professional ethics should know that there are many works on moral theory. The following list, divided into primary works and secondary sources that serve to explain primary works, may perform this purpose, as well as serving as a guide for those who would like to do further study in moral theory.

Primary Sources

Adler, Mortimer J. *A Dialectic of Morals*. Notre Dame, Indiana: The Review of Politics, University of Notre Dame Press, 1941.

Adler, Mortimer J. *The Time of Our Lives: The Ethics of Common Sense*. New York: Holt, Rinehart and Winston, 1970. A basic presentation of common sense morality.

Aquinas, Thomas. *Summa Contra Gentiles*. There are many translations available of the two *Summas* of Aquinas. This work provides at times a more accessible understanding of natural law than its more famous counterpart, the *Summa Theologica*.

Aquinas, Thomas. *Summa Theologica*. Although this is primarily a theological work of encyclopedic length, it represents the classic statement of natural law ethical thought with a careful treatment of virtue ethics.

Aristotle. *Nicomachean Ethics.* There are numerous translations of this classic work by Aristotle which represents the Greek formulation of natural law ethics, including those of T.E. Irwin and W.D. Ross.

Augustine. *City of God.* There are several translations of Augustine's work available in English. One of Augustine's most famous works, this account depicts a heavily fideistic account of morality. It is only through the grace of God that humans can attain goodness.

Augustine. *Confessions.* A new translation by Henry Chadwick. Oxford: Oxford University Press, 1991. This classic autobiographical account depicts the need for faith and the role of grace in human morality.

Augustine. *On Free Will.* This work is the first clear defense of the freedom of the will in Western thought.

Avicenna. *The Book of Salvation.* The classic Islamic development of Aristotle's natural law theory.

Ayer, A.J. *Language, Truth and Logic.* Second edition. New York: Dover Publications, Inc., 1946. The classic statement of the emotivist theory of the logical positivist. According to Ayer moral propositions cannot be supported by facts, and so are simply statements of emotion.

Baier, Kurt. *The Moral Point of View.* Ithica, New York: Cornell University Press, 1958. A contemporary statement of a deontological ethic. Baier sees morality in terms of social control.

Beach, Waldo and Neibuhr, H. Richard, editors. *Christian Ethics.* New York: Ronald Press, 1955.

Bellah, Robert, et. al. *Habits of the Heart.* New York: Perennial Library, 1985. A very accessible study of individualism and community, and how these two effect the way Americans talk and think about the moral life.

Bellah, Robert, et. al. *The Good Society.* New York: Alfred A. Knopf, 1991. Continues the themes of *Habits of the Heart,* especially the search for an understanding of the common good.

Bentham, Jeremy. *An Introduction to the Principles of Morals and Legislation.* New York: Russell & Russell, Inc., Publishers, 1962. Jeremy Bentham is generally considered to be one of the founders of Utilitarian moral theory.

Blum, Lawrence A. *Friendship, Altruism and Morality.* Routledge & Kegan Paul, 1980. A groundbreaking piece in contemporary theories of virtue ethics. Includes thoughtful critiques of Kantian and utilitarian ethical theories.

Bok, Sissela. *Lying: Moral Choice in Public and Private Life.* New York: Pantheon Books, 1978.

Bourke, Vernon J. *Ethics.* Second edition. New York: The Macmillan Company, 1966. An explanation and development of natural law ethics in the Thomistic tradition.

Brandt, Richard B. *A Theory of the Good and the Right.* Oxford University Press, 1979. An advanced look at the role of values in utilitarian morality.

Brody, Baruch. *Moral Rules and Particular Circumstances.* Englewood Cliffs, New Jersey: Prentice Hall, Inc., 1970.

Brunner, Emil. *The Divine Imperative.* Translated by Oliver Wyon. Philadelphia: The Westminster Press, 1947. A theory of divine command where right actions are those performed in obedience to God's will.

Butler, Joseph. *Sermons.* From *The Works of Joseph Butler*, vol. 2. Oxford: The Clarendon Press, 1874. Reacting primarily against psychological egoists, Butler espouses a conscience-oriented theory of morality.

Confucius. *The Analects of Confucius.* A classic piece in Chinese philosophy which seeks the goal of human life, the ideal relationship of *jen*, through *tao*, the right way.

Dewey, John. *Human Nature and Conduct.* New York: Henry Holt & Company, 1922. An approach to morality offered by the famous American pragmatist. This considers morality to be something invented to meet specific situations, and is termed a kind of instrumentalist approach to ethics.

Donagan, Alan. *The Theory of Morality.* Chicago: University of Chicago Press, 1977. A clear statement of traditional morality. Donagan emphasizes the principle of respect for persons.

Epictetus. *The Encheiridion.* In *The Discourses*, Vol. II. Translated by W.A. Oldfather, Cambridge, Massachusetts: Harvard University Press. The classic exposition of Roman Stoicism.

Epicurus. *The Extant Remains.* Translated by C. Bailey. Oxford: Clarendon Press, 1926. This work contains Epicurus's classic development of ethical hedonism.

Finnis, John. *Natural Law and Natural Rights.* Oxford: Oxford University Press, 1980. A contemporary treatment of natural law ethics.

Fletcher, Joseph. *Moral Responsibility.* Philadelphia: The Westminster Press, 1967. Fletcher offers a theory of situation ethics.

Fletcher, Joseph. *Situation Ethics.* Philadelphia: The Westminster Press, 1966. A treatment of the approach to ethical decision making known as situation ethics.

Flew, Antony. *Evolutionary Ethics.* New York: St. Martin's Press, 1967.

Foot, Philippa. *Virtues and Vices*. Oxford: Basil Blackwell, 1978. A collection of articles by one of the foremost proponents of virtue ethics.

Fox, Marvin, editor. *Modern Jewish Ethics: Theory and Practice*. Columbus, Ohio: State University Press, 1975. A clear statement of modern Jewish approaches to ethics.

Frankena, William K. *Ethics*. New edition. Englewood Cliffs, New Jersey: Prentice-Hall, 1974.

Fuchs, Josef. *Christian Ethics in a Secular Arena*. Washington, D.C.: Georgetown University Press, 1984. A contemporary Catholic theologian who espouses a proportionalist approach to ethics.

Fudenberg, Drew and Tirole, Jean. *Game Theory*. Cambridge, Massachusetts: MIT Press, 1991. An in depth look at contemporary game theory.

Gauthier, David. *Morals by Agreement*. New York: Oxford University Press, 1986. A defense of contractarianism that relies heavily on game theory.

Gert, Bernard. *The Moral Rules: A New Rational Foundation for Morality*. New York: Harper & Row, 1973. Defends a rationalist approach to ethics.

Gewirth, Alan. *Reason and Morality*. Chicago: University of Chicago Press, 1978. A contemporary theory of deontological ethics.

Gilligan, Carol. *In Another Voice: Psychological Theory and Women's Development*. Cambridge: Harvard University Press, 1982. Criticizing Kohlberg from a female perspective, Gilligan presents the ethic of care as an alternative to rule based ethics.

Gilson, Etienne. *Moral Values and Moral Life*. Hamden, Connecticut: The Shoe String Press, Inc., 1961. A good modern development of natural law ethics by one of the twentieth century's most famous Thomists.

Gordis, Robert. *Judaic Ethics for a Lawless World*. New York: Jewish Theological Seminary of America, 1986. A basic exposition of the Judaic approach to ethics in the contemporary arena.

Goossens, Charles. *Towards a Theory of Relativity of Truth in Morality and Religion*. Lewiston, New York: E. Mellon Press, 1990. An explanation and defense of relativism.

Hare, R.M. *Freedom and Reason*. New York: Oxford University Press, Inc., 1965. Hare develops a form of ethical reasoning he names universal prescriptivism.

Hare, R.M. *The Language of Morals*. New edition. London: Oxford University Press, 1973. Another work of Hare's explaining his theory of universal prescriptivism.

Hegel, George W.F. *Philosophy of Right*. Oxford: The Clarendon Press, 1949.

Hobbes, Thomas. *Leviathan*. Oxford: The Clarendon Press, 1909. Hobbes develops a theory of psychological egoism where morality is determined by primarily by power; specifically, political power. Hobbes's theory also contains some of the earliest elements of social contract theory.

Hume, David. *Inquiry Concerning the Principles of Morals*. Indianapolis: Bobbs-Merrill Company, Inc., 1957. Hume's development of the ethical theory of emotivism.

Hume, David. *Treatise of Human Nature*. Oxford: The Clarendon Press, 1888. Hume's classic work which contains the elements of his emotivist theory of ethics.

Idziak, J.M. *Divine Command Morality*. Lewiston, New York: Edwin Mellon Press, 1986. A recent work on divine command ethics.

James, William. *Pragmatism.* New York: Longmans, Green & Company, Inc., 1907. Famous American pragmatist who argues against moral absolutes.

Jonsen, Albert R., and Stephen Toulmin. *The Abuse of Casuistry: A History of Moral Reasoning*. (Berkeley and Los Angeles: University of California Press, 1988).

Kant, Immanuel. *Critique of Practical Reason.* Translated by Lewis White Beck. Indianapolis: The Bobbs-Merrill Company, 1956. Kant's formulation of a deontological, *a priori*, duty-oriented ethics.

Kant, Immanuel. *Foundations of the Metaphysics of Morals*. Translated by Lewis White Beck. New York: The Liberal Arts Press, 1959. (Other translations are available.) Kant sets out the fundamental principles of his ethical theory in this work which acts as a prolegomena to his fuller ethical theory in the *Critique of Practical Reason* and *The Metaphysics of Morals*.

Kant, Immanuel. *Lectures on Ethics*. Edited by P. Menzer. New York: Harper & Row, 1963. More of Kant's deontological ethics of duty, though this contains a fuller discussion of virtue.

Kierkegaard, Soren. *Either/Or*. Several translations available. Contrasts a self-interested approach to life with a duty ethic.

Kierkegaard, Soren. *Fear and Trembling*. Criticizes the limits of a universal rational ethic in light of the importance of the individual.

Kohlberg, Lawrence. *Essays on Moral Development*. San Francisco: Harper & Row, 1981. Kohlberg, Lawrence and Hewer, A. *Moral Stages*. New York: S. Karger, AG, 1983. The psychological theory which recognizes conscience-based action on moral principles as the highest level of moral development.

Kohlberg, Lawrence. *The Philosophy of Moral Development.* New York: Harper & Row, 1981. His chapter on the fact/value problem is important for some of our arguments in chapters one and two.

Kohlberg, Lawrence, *The Psychology of Moral Development.* New York: Harper & Row, 1984.

Locke, John. *A Letter Concerning ReligiousToleration.* New York: Appleton-Century-Crogts, 1937. This work espouses the theory of natural human rights.

Locke, John. *Two Treatises of Government.* New York: Hafner Publishing Company, Inc., 1947. Locke's most famous works which develop his theory of natural rights.

McCormick, Richard A. *Ambiguity in Moral Choice.* Milwaukee: Marquette University Press, 1973. A work by a Catholic theologian who argues for proportionalism.

MacIntyre, Alasdair. *After Virtue.* Second edition. South Bend, Indiana: Notre Dame University Press, 1984. An important contemporary work on virtue ethics.

Mackie, J.L. *Ethics: Inventing Right and Wrong.* New York: Penguin Books, 1977. Mackie offers a theory of ethical relativism.

Mackie, J.L. *Reason and Values.* Oxford: Clarendon Press, 1985. Another statement of Mackie's development of ethical relativism.

Manning, Rita C. *Speaking from the Heart: A Feminist Perspective on Ethics.* Lanham, Maryland: Rowman & Littlefield, 1992. Manning offers a feminist statement and defense of an ethic of care.

Marcus Aurelius. *The Meditations.* The reflections of Marcus Aurelius which focus mainly upon his version of Stoic ethics.

Maritain, Jacques. *The Person and the Common Good.* New York: Charles Scribner's Sons, 1947. A short work that lays out the basic natural law understanding of the common good.

Maritain, Jacques. *The Rights of Man and Natural Law.* Translated by Doris C. Anson. New York: Gordian Press, Inc., 1971. An important work in modern natural law theory by the famous French Thomist.

Mill, John Stuart. *On Liberty.* From *On Liberty and Other Essays.* Edited by John Gray. Oxford: Oxford University Press, 1991. An important treatment on the role of freedom in morality from the great utilitarian thinker.

Mill, John Stuart. *Utilitarianism.* Edited by Oskar Piest. Indianapolis: The Bobbs-Merrill Company, inc., 1957. Mill is commonly regarded to be the most important utilitarian theorist. His theory attempted to ameliorate the extreme hedonism of Bentham's theory.

Moore, G.E. *Ethics.* London: Oxford University Press, 1912. An analytic exposition of ideal utilitarianism which reflects Moore's insistence that other goods besides pleasure are desirable.

Moore, G.E. *Principia Ethica.* Cambridge University Press, 1903. The seminal work in modern discussions of meta-ethics. This work also offers an exposition of Moore's ethics which has become known as ideal utilitarianism.

Neibuhr, H. Richard. *The Responsible Self.* New York: Harper & Row, 1963.

Neibuhr, Reinhold. *An Interpretation of Christian Ethics.* Cleveland: World, 1956. An accessible statement of a specifically Christian approach to ethical action.

Nielsen, Kai. *Ethics Without God.* Pemberton Books, 1973. A defense of a utilitarian secular morality.

Noddings, Nel. *Caring, a Feminist Approach to Ethics and Moral Education*. Berkeley: University of California Press, 1984. A feminist development of the ethics of caring.

Olson, Robert. *The Morality of Self-Interest*. New York: Harcourt, Brace & World, Inc., 1965. A theory of moral egoism.

Piaget, Jean. *The Moral Judgement of the Child*. New York: Free Press, 1965. A psychological study of the development of moral judgements.

Pieper, Josef. *The Four Cardinal Virtues*. Notre Dame, Indiana: University of Notre Dame Press, 1967.

Plato. *Gorgias, Meno, Philebus*. Platonic dialogues concerned with ethics.

Plato. *The Republic*. Plato's classic dialogue on moral and political philosophy which answers the question of 'why be just?' with a theory of the need for human psychic harmony.

Quinn, Philip. *Divine Commands and Moral Requirements*. Clarendon Press, 1978. An exposition of the divine command theory of ethics.

Quinton, Anthony. *Utilitarian Ethics*. London: The MacMillan Company, 1973. A good explanation and defense of classical utilitarian theory.

Rand, Ayn. *The Virtue of Selfishness: A New Concept of Egoism*. New York: New American Library, 1964. Rand presents a theory of egoism which is termed rational selfishness.

Rawls, John. *A Theory of Justice*. Cambridge, Massachusetts: Harvard University Press, 1971. A theory of fairness based upon a social contract of rational beings. It draws upon Kantian principles without explicitly grounding the theory on them.

Ross, W.D. *The Right and the Good*. Oxford University Press, 1930. A twentieth century development of deontological ethics in response to utilitarianism.

Rousseau, Jean Jacques. *The Social Contract*. New York: Hafner Publishing Company, Inc., 1947. An early development of social contract theory whereby all human rights are the result of some form of social agreement.

Sartre, Jean-Paul. *Being and Nothingness*. New York: Philosophical Library, Inc., 1956. An existentialist work which upholds human freedom as the highest value of human persons. Although this does not offer a specific treatment of ethics, it gives insight into the existentialist understanding of human responsibility for action.

Smith, Adam. *The Theory of Moral Sentiments*. New Rochelle, New York: Arlington House, Inc., 1969. Smith's version of emotivism which develops the idea of moral sympathies.

Spinoza, Baruch. *Ethics*. From the *Chief Works of Spinoza*. New York: Dover Publications, Inc., 1951. A rationalist account of ethics from the perspective of a materialist who holds that human reason is capable, of its own, to attain perfection in God.

Stevenson, C.L. *Ethics and Language*. New Haven: Yale University Press, 1944. A careful and thoughtful formulation and defense of emotivism.

Taylor, Richard. *Good and Evil: A New Direction*. New York: The Macmillan Company, 1970.

Tong, Rosemarie. *Feminine and Feminist Ethics*. Wadsworth, 1993. Tong draws out distinctions between the older 'feminine' and the newer 'feminist' theories of ethics.

Toulmin, Stephen. *An Examination of the Place of Reason in Ethics*. London: Cambridge University Press, 1950. The first explicit defense of rule utilitarianism.

Secondary Sources

Anderson, Thomas. *The Foundation and Structure of Sartrean Ethics*. Laurence: Regents Press of Kansas, 1979. An exposition of Sartre's existentialist ethical thinking.

Aquinas, Thomas. *Commentary on the Nicomachean Ethics*. Translated by C.I. Litzinger. Chicago: Regnery Press, 1964. An excellent commentary on Aristotle's ethics.

Baker, James T. *Ayn Rand*. Boston: Twayne Publishers, 1987. A study of Rand's theory of rational selfishness.

Beck, Lewis White. *A Commentary on Kant's Critique of Practical Reason*. Chicago: The University of Chicago Press, 1960. An excellent commentary by one of Kant's foremost translators

Blocker, H.G. and Smith, E.H., editors. *John Rawls' Theory of Social Justice: An Introduction*. Athens: Ohio University Press, 1980. A collection of essays on Rawls theory of justice as fairness.

Bourke, Vernon J. *Joy in Augustine's Ethics*. Villanova, Pennsylvania: Villanova University, 1979. A useful study of Augustine's ethical approach.

Brennan, Bernard P. *The Ethics of William James*. New York: Bookman Associates, 1961. Captures the elements of the famous pragmatist's ethical thinking.

Colman, John. *John Locke's Moral Philosophy*. Edinburgh: Edinburgh University Press, 1983. A good exposition of Locke's moral thinking.

Copleston, Frederick. *A History of Philosophy*. New York: Doubleday, 1985. An incomparable exposition of Western philosophy.

Danto, Arthur Coleman. *Mysticism and Morality: Oriental Thought and Moral Philosophy.* New York: Columbia University Press, 1987. A good resource to understanding Eastern philosophy and its ethical views.

Dharmasiri, Gunapala. *Fundamentals of Buddhist Ethics.* Antioch, California: Golden Leaves, 1989. A guide to the ethical thinking of Buddhism.

Duncan-Jones, A.E. *Butler's Moral Philosophy.* Baltimore: Penguin Books, 1952. An interesting study and critique of Butler's ethical theory.

Foot, Philippa, editor. *Theories of Ethics.* Oxford: Oxford University Press, 1976. An excellent collection of articles on moral theories and the nature of moral judgment.

Gilson, Etienne. *The Christian Philosophy of St. Augustine.* New York: Random House, Inc., 1960. An excellent treatment of the philosophy and moral thought of St. Augustine.

Gilson, Etienne. *The Christian Philosophy of St. Thomas Aquinas.* New York: Random House, Inc., 1956. An excellent guide to the philosophy and ethics of Aquinas.

Gouinlock, J. *John Dewey's Philosophy of Value.* New York: Humanities Press, 1972. This book examines the moral theory of John Dewey within the context of his pragmatic philosophy.

Graham, A.C. *Disputers of the Tao: Philosophical Argument in Ancient China.* Peru, Illinois: Open Court Publishing Company, 1989. An interesting account of the philosophical schools of ancient China.

Hampton, Jean. *Hobbes and the Social Contract Tradition.* New York: Cambridge University Press, 1986. An interesting explanation/critique/defense of Hobbes's theory of social contract.

Hicks, R.D. *Stoic and Epicurean.* New York: Russell & Russell,1962. A survey of their philosophies.

Hooper, J. Leon. *The Ethics of Discourse: John Courtney Murray's Social Philosophy.* Washington, D.C.: Georgetown University Press, 1986. A contemporary study of discourse ethics.

Hovannisian, Richard G., editor. *Ethics in Islam.* Malibu: Undena, 1985.

Irwin, Terence. *Plato's Moral Theory: The Early and Middle Dialogues.* Oxford: The Clarendon Press, 1977. An excellent treatment of the development of Platonic ethics.

Ivanhoe, Philip J. *Ethics in the Confucian Tradition: The Thought of Menicus and Wang Yang-ming.* Atlanta, Georgia: Scholars Press, 1990. A helpful study for understanding Eastern philosophy.

Johnson, Oliver. *Rightness and Goodness.* The Hague: Martinus Nijhoff, 1959. A careful and critical study of deontological theories of ethics.

Kavka, G. *Hobbesian Moral and Political Theory.* Princeton: Princeton University Press, 1986. A thorough exploration of Hobbes's thought.

Kerner, George C. *Three Philosophical Moralists: Mill, Kant, and Sartre.* A unique analysis of these three philosophers. In the end, the author sides with Sartre that there are no objective answers to morality -- only questions.

Ladd, J. *Ethical Relativism.* Wadsworth, 1973. A collection of essays on the subject of relativism.

Long, Edward Leroy. *A Survey of Christian Ethics.* New York: Oxford University Press, 1967. A helpful study for understanding ethics in a Christian context.

Lukes, Steven. *Marxism and Morality*. Oxford: Oxford University Press, 1985. The author examines Marxism's connection with morality.

MacIntyre, Alasdair. *A Short History of Ethics*. New York: The MacMillan Company, 1966. An accessible treatment of the history of philosophical ethics in the Western tradition.

Mackie, J.L. *Hume's Moral Theory*. London: Routledge & Kegan Paul, 1980. A helpful explanation of Hume's ethics.

Miller, Harlan B., and Williams, William, editors. *The Limits of Utilitarianism*. University of Minnesota Press, 1982. A collection of articles for advanced study.

Nell, Onora. *Acting on Principle: An Essay on Kantian Ethics*. New York: Columbia University Press, 1975. A good explanation of Kant's deontological, duty-oriented ethics.

Nielsen, Kai and Patten, S.C., editors. *Marx and Morality*. Guelph, Ontario: Canadian Association for Publishing Philosophy, 1981. A collection of essays dealing with Marx's ethical views.

O'Connor, D.J. *Aquinas and Natural Law*. London: MacMillan, 1968. A critical analysis of the natural law tradition of St. Thomas Aquinas.

Outka, Gene and Reeder, J.P., editors. *Religion and Morality: A Collection of Essays*. Anchor Books, 1973. Contains articles on the relationship between faith and ethics.

Paton, H.J. *The Categorical Imperative*. Chicago: Chicago University Press, 1948. A classic exposition of Kantian ethics.

Plamenatz, J. *The English Utilitarians*. Oxford: Blackwell, 1966. A critical study of the English tradition of utilitarian ethics.

Pojman, Louis, editor. *Ethical Theory: Classical and Contemporary Readings*. Wadsworth, 1989. A helpful anthology of readings in ethics.

Porter, Jean. *The Recovery of Virtue: The Relevance of Aquinas for Christian Ethics*. Louisville, Kentucky: John Knox Press, 1990. An examination of the role and importance of virtue in Aquinas's natural law ethics.

Regan, Tom. *Bloomsbury's Prophet: G.E. Moore and the Development of His Moral Philosophy*. Philadelphia: Temple University Press, 1986. A useful guide to understanding the ethical views of Moore.

Rohatyn, D. *The Reluctant Naturalist*. Lanham: University Press of America, 1987. An interesting view of Moore's ethical theory.

Rorty, Amelie Oksenberg, editor. *Essays on Aristotle's Ethics*. Berkeley, California: University of California Press, 1980. A collection of essays which serve as a commentary on Aristotle's *Nicomachean Ethics*.

Schaefer, D.L. *Justice or Tyranny?* Port Washington, New York: Kennikat Press, 1979. Schaefer takes issue with Rawls over his theory of 'fairness.'

Scheffler, Samuel, editor. *Consequentialism and Its Critics*. Oxford: Oxford University Press, 1988. An interesting anthology of pro and con articles on consequentialist theories of ethics.

Seanor, Douglas and Fotion, N. *Hare and Critics: Essays on Moral Thinking*. Oxford: Oxford University Press, 1988. A collection of essays on Hare's *Moral Thinking* with Hare's responses.

Semmel, B. *John Stuart Mill and the Pursuit of Virtue*. New Haven: Yale University Press, 1984. A contemporary explanation and interpretation of Mill's utilitarianism.

Stroud, B. *Hume*. London: Routledge & Kegan Paul, 1977. An interpretation of the work of David Hume, including an exposition of his ethical theory.

Warnock, Mary. *Ethics Since 1900*. Oxford: Oxford University Press, 1960. A short and accessible study of ethics in the twentieth century.

Warnock, Mary. *Existentialist Ethics*. New York: St. Martin's Press, 1967. A guide to existentialist moral philosophy.

White, A.R. *G. E. Moore*. Oxford: Blackwell, 1958. A good exposition of Moore's philosophy, including an analytic study of his moral theory.

Wood, Allen W. *Hegel's Ethical Thought*. New York: Cambridge University Press, 1990. An explanation of Hegel's approach to morality.

Xenakis, I. *Epictetus*. The Hague: Martinus Nijhoff, 1969. Contains a helpful commentary on the stoic ethics of Epictetus.

Appendix 5

Some Works that Contain Case Studies

Accounting Professions

Cottell, Philip G., Jr. and Perlin, Terry M. *Accounting Ethics: A Practical Guide for Professionals*. New York: Quorum Books, 1990. Covers several important ethical topics accountants must face and offers two case studies at the end of each chapter.

Windal, Floyd W. *Ethics and the Accountant: Text and Cases*. Englewood Cliffs, New Jersey: Prentice-Hall, 1991. Highlights the professional role of the accountant. Each chapter ends with a number of cases for the reader's consideration.

Business Professions

Beauchamp, Tom L. *Case Studies in Business, Society, and Ethics*. Third edition. Englewood Cliffs, New Jersey: Prentice-Hall, 1993. Contains 35 contemporary cases of actual situations with detailed study and explanation.

Beauchamp, Tom L. and Bowie, Norman. *Ethical Theory and Business*. Fourth edition. Englewood Cliffs, New Jersey: Prentice-Hall, 1993. Primarily a topical collection of articles supported by thought-provoking case studies

Boatright, John R. *Ethics and the Conduct of Business.* Englewood Cliffs, New Jersey: Prentice-Hall, 1993. Focuses on issues in business ethics, but interweaves abundant case studies as a basis for discussion.

Cederblom, Jerry and Dougherty, Charles. *Ethics at Work.* Wadsworth, 1990. Gives a nontechnical survey of ethical theories, followed by 27 cases that cover a wide range of problems encountered in the workplace.

Desjardins, Joseph and McCall, John. *Contemporary Issues in Business Ethics.* Second edition. Wadsworth, 1990. Primarily uses an issues approach with a discussion of various moral theories and essays on various issues, though it also includes 60 brief cases.

Donaldson, Thomas and Werhane, Patricia. *Ethical Issues in Business.* Fourth edition. Englewood Cliffs, New Jersey: Prentice-Hall, 1993. This book is essentially a collection of essays on issues, though there is one case study included for each issue discussed.

Donaldson, Thomas and Gini, A.R. *Case Studies in Business Ethics.* Third edition. Englewood Cliffs, New Jersey: Prentice-Hall, 1993. A good collection of business cases.

Goodpaster, Kenneth E. *Ethics in Management: Harvard Business School Case Studies.* Boston: Harvard Business School, 1984.

Hilgert, Raymond L. et. al. *Cases and Experimental Exercises in Human Resource Management.* Boston: Allyn & Bacon, 1990. A useful collection.

Hoffman, W. Michael and Moore, Jennifer Mills. *Business Ethics: Readings and Cases in Corporate Morality.* Second edition. New York: McGraw-Hill, 1990. Offers a number of interesting cases.

Iannone, A. Pablo. *Contemporary Moral Controversies in Business*. Oxford: Oxford University Press, 1989. Primarily an anthology of articles, though a number of cases that have gone to court are included.

Jennings, Marianne, M. *Case Studies in Business Ethics*. St. Paul: West Publishing Co., 1993. Contains over 120 cases covering many companies and many issues in business ethics. The description of each case is very brief, often less than one page. Bibliographical information is included for those who want to pursue a more detailed analysis of a specific case.

Molander, Earl A. and Arthur, David L. *Responsive Capitalism: Case Studies in Corporate Social Conduct*. New York: McGraw-Hill, 1980. Case studies help highlight the responsibility of today's corporations.

Partridge, Scott H. *Cases in Business and Society*. Englewood Cliffs, New Jersey: Prentice Hall, 1982. A helpful collection of cases.

Pfeiffer, Raymond S. and Forsberg, Ralph P. Forsberg. Ethics on the Job. Belmont, CA: Wadsworth, 1993. Contains forty cases, about two pages long each, on a wide range of job related topics, including hiring, firing, employee and employer obligations, and problems with co-workers.

Shaw, William H. *Business Ethics*. Wadsworth, 1991. Includes thirty-one practical case studies, designed primarily for the undergraduate level.

Shaw, William H. and Barry, Vincent. *Moral Issues in Business*. Fifth edition. Wadsworth, 1992. A combination text/anthology/casebook that includes over 40 cases.

Velasquez, Manuel G. *Business Ethics: Concepts and Cases*. Third edition. Englewood Cliffs, New Jersey: Prentice-Hall, 1982, 1988. Discusses various aspects of business ethics followed by case studies.

Westin, Alan. *Whistle-blowing!* New York: McGraw Hill, 1981. Includes case studies of a handful of people from various businesses involved in whistlblowing cases.

Westin, Alan F. and Aram, John D. *Managerial Dilemmas: Cases in Social, Legal and Technological Change.* Cambridge, Massachusetts: Ballinger, 1988. Offers case studies relating to a wide range of areas in business ethics.

Williams, Oliver F. and Houck, John W. *A Virtuous Life in Business.* Published in cooperation with the Notre Dame Center for Ethics and Religious Values in Business. Lanham, Maryland: Rowman & Littlefield Publishers, 1992. Covers recent cases in the ethics of business management.

Engineering Professions

Fielder, John H. and Birsch, Douglas. *The DC-10 Case, A Study in Applied Ethics, Technology and Society.* Albany: SUNY Press, 1992. A detailed study of the DC-10 from its early design through its major crashes in 1974, '79 and '89. Provides a good way to get at many ethical questions in engineering and aerospace.

Johnson, Deborah G. *Ethical Issues in Engineering.* Englewood Cliffs, New Jersey: Prentice-Hall, 1991. Case readings on ethical issues confronting the profession of engineering.

Pinkus, Rosa Lynn, Shuman, Larry J. Hummon, Norman, and Wolfe, Harvey. *The Ethical Behavior of Engineers: An Analysis of the Space Shuttle Program.* National Science Foundation Grant, University of Pittsburgh, 1991. Examines the case of the space shuttle in ten individual sections.

Schaub, James H. and Pavlovic, Karl, with M.D. Morris. *Engineering Professionalism and Ethics*. New York: John Wiley & Sons, 1983. An anthology of readings in engineering ethics with cases studies interwoven throughout.

Legal Professions

Bellow, Gary and Moulton, Bea. *Ethics and Professional Responsibility*. Westbury, New York: Foundation Press, 1981. A collection of cases in legal ethics.

Davis, Michael and Elliston, Frederick A., editors. *Ethics and the Legal Profession*. Buffalo, New York: Prometheus Books, 1986. This book draws both from the legal tradition and the philosophical tradition to offer a guide to legal ethics, and is accompanied by a number of hypothetical cases to encourage discussion.

Greenawalt, Kent. *Conflicts of Law and Morality*. Oxford: Oxford University Press, 1987. This text lays out a wide spectrum of case studies.

Heyman and Lance Liebman. *The Social Responsibilities of Lawyers: Case Studies*. Westbury, New York: Foundation Press, 1988. A collection of case studies in the legal profession.

Morgan, Thomas D. and Rotunda, Richard D. *Professional Responsibility*. Fourth edition. Westbury, New York: Foundation Press, 1987. Cases relating to professional responsibility for lawyers.

Pirsig, Maynard E. and Kirwin, Kenneth F. *Cases and Materials on Professional Responsibility*. Third edition. St. Paul, Minnesota: West Publishing Company, 1976. A casebook and resource guide for ethics in the legal profession.

Redlich, Norman. *Professional Responsibility: A Problem Approach.* Boston, Massachusetts: Little, Brown, and Company, 1976. An approach to legal ethics using case studies.

Schwartz, Murray L. *Lawyers and the Legal Profession: Cases and Materials.* New York: Bobbs-Merrill, 1979. A good collection of cases and resources for ethics in the legal profession.

Media Professions

Christians, Clifford G., Rotzoll, Kim B. and Fackler, Mark. *Media Ethics: Cases and Moral Reasoning.* New York: Longman, 1983. 76 cases studies and commentaries covering news, advertising, and entertainment.

Flint, Leon Nelson. *The Conscience of the Newspaper.* New York: D. Appleton, 1925. Illustrates actual cases from press activities.

Heine, William C. *Journalism Ethics: A Case Book.* London: University of Western Ontario Library, 1975. 12 case studies from the Britain and Ontario Press Councils.

Hulteng, John L. *Playing it Straight: A Practical Discussion of the Ethical Principles of ASNE.* Chester, Connecticut: Globe Pequot Press, 1981. An examination of the principles of the American Society of Newspaper Editors through case studies.

Klaidman, Stephen and Beauchamp, Tom L. *The Virtuous Journalist.* Oxford: Oxford University Press, 1987. A reflective account of ethics in journalism using concrete examples of recent news stories.

McCulloch, Frank, editor. *Drawing the Line.* Washington, D.C.: American Society of Newspaper Editors, 1984. 31 case tudies written by editors.

Meyer, Philip. *Editors, Publishers and Newspaper Ethics*. Washington, D.C.: American Society of Newspaper Editors, 1983. Covers selected ethical issues and case studies.

Medical Professions

Ackerman, Terrence F. and Strong, Carson. *A Casebook of Medical Ethics*. Oxford: Oxford University Press, 1989. Primarily an analysis of real-life cases which are developed in detail to indicate the complexity of medical issues.

Benjamin, Martin and Curtis, Joy. *Ethics in Nursing*. Third edition. Oxford: Oxford University Press, 1991. Written by a nurse and a philosopher, this work combines real life case studies with the methods of philosophical ethics.

Brody, Baruch A. and Englehardt, H. Tristam. *Bioethics: Readings and Cases*. Englewood Cliffs, New Jersey: Prentice-Hall, 1987. A helpful collection of cases.

Freeman, John M. and McDonnell, Kevin. *Tough Decisions: A Casebook in Medical Ethics*. Oxford: Oxford University Press, 1987. A Collection of vivid cases described in clinical terms. These cases are interesting, because the cases unfold to show how each decision leads to a new set of issues and often a new decision. Complements our work well.

Guillemin, Jeanne Harley and Holmstrom, Lynda Lytle. *Mixed Blesssings: Intensive Care for Newborns*. Oxford: Oxford University Press, 1986. Very specific case studies are presented regarding NICUs, but issues in hospital research are also addressed.

Hull, Richard T. *Ethical Issues in the New Reproductive Technologies*. Wadsworth, 1990. Each chapter begins with concrete case studies which cover a wide range of issues.

Lincourt, John. *Ethics Without a Net: A case Workbook in Bioethics.* Dubuque: Kendall/Hunt, 1991. Fifteen cases based on actual clinical experiences. This is a nice workbook and a good complement to our text; the cases provide sufficient detail and then lead the student through a series of questions that encourage the student to focus on the ethically relevant issues.

Munson, Ronald. *Intervention and Reflection: Basic Issues in Medical Ethics*. Fourth edition. Wadsworth, 1992. Contains over 80 decision making cases relating to issues faced in the medical profession today.

Pence, Gregory. *Classic Cases in Medical Ethics*. New York: McGraw Hill, 1990. Includes famous hard cases in a number of areas in medical ethics.

Rachels, James. *The End of Life: Euthanasia and Morality*. Oxford: Oxford University Press, 1986. Examines the arguments for and against euthanasia with an analysis of specific case studies.

Shannon, Thomas and Manfra, JoAnn. *Law and Bioethics: Selected Cases*. Ramsey, New Jersey: Paulist Press, 1981. A helpful collection of cases on bioethics.

Shapiro, Michael H. and Spece, Roy G., Jr. *Cases, Materials, and Problems on Bioethics and Law*. St. Paul, Minnesota: West Publishing Company, 1981. A good resource on biomedical ethics containing case studies.

Veatch, Robert M. *Case Studies in Medical Ethics*. Cambridge, Massachusetts: Harvard University Press, 1977. Includes over 100 cases in medical ethics.

Wojcik, Jan. *Muted Consent: A Casebook in Modern Medical Ethics*. West Lafayette, Indiana: Purdue Research Foundation, 1978. A very useful casebook.

Zucker, Arthur, Borchert, Donald and Stewart, David. *Medical Ethics: A Reader*. Englewood Cliffs, New Jersey: Prentice Hall, 1992. An anthology of classic readings in medical ethics supplemented with case studies.

Psychological Professions

American Psychological Association. *Casebook on Ethical Standards of Psychologists*. Revised edition. New York: A.P.A., 1987. A good collection of case studies from the A.P.A.

Keith-Spiegel, Patricia. *Ethics in Psychology: Professional Standards and Cases*. New York: Random House, 1985. Developed around the ethics code, this collection contains more than 300 vignettes based on actual cases.

Public Service Professions

Bowman, James S. and Elliston, Frederick A. *Ethics, Government, and Public Policy: A Reference Guide*. New York: Greenwood Press, 1988. A helpful resource on ethical issues in politics with interwoven cases.

Gutman, Amy and Thompson, Dennis, editors. *Ethics and Politics: Cases and Comments*. Chicago: Nelson-Hall, 1984. A good collection of case studies in political ethics.

Lewis, Carol W. *The Ethics Challenge in Public Service: A Problem-Solving Guide*. San Francisco: Jossey-Bass Publishers, 1991. This book offers techniques for solving problems faced by those in public service. It contains a number of interesting cases interwoven throughout the text.

Mertins, Herman, Jr. and Hennigan, Patrick J., editors. *Applying Professional Standards and Ethics in 1980's: A Workbook and Study Guide for Public Administrators*. Second edition. Washington, D.C.: American Society for Public Administration, 1982. A good resource for public servants with case studies.

Timmins, W.M. *A Casebook of Public Ethics & Issues*. Pacific Grove, California: Brooks/Cole, 1990. A resource book of case studies for use in public service professions.

Scientific Professions

Reagan, Charles E. *Ethics for Scientific Researchers*. Second Edition. Springfield, Illinois: Charles C. Thomas, Publisher, 1971. Contains a basic introduction to ethics, followed by a casebook of issues in scientific research.

General Works with Case Studies

Applebaum, David and Lawton, Sarah V. *Ethics and the Professions*. Englewood Cliffs, New Jersey: Prentice-Hall, 1990. Contains numerous decision-making scenarios covering a wide spectrum of professional ethics.

Baum, Robert, editor. *Ethical Arguments for Analysis*. Revised edition. New York: Holt, Rinehart and Winston, 1979. An interesting array of cases to consider taken from every day life.

Callahan, Joan C., editor. *Ethical Issues in Professional Life*. Oxford: Oxford University Press, 1988. Presents an interdisciplinary approach to ethics with case studies covering a wide range of professions.

Harris, C.E., JR. *Applying Moral Theories*. Second edition. Wadsworth, 1992. A guide to ethical theories which makes use of case studies.